the crying shore

melissa maclellan

Published by Dolman Scott Ltd 2019

Copyright © 2019 Melissa MacLellan

The author asserts the moral right under the Copyright, Designs and Patents Act 1988 to be identified as the author of this work. All rights reserved. No part of this publication may be reproduced, stored in a retrieval system, or transmitted, in any form or by any means without the prior written consent of the author, nor be otherwise circulated in any form of binding or cover, other than that in which it is published and without a similar condition being imposed on the subsequent purchaser.

ISBN: 978-1-911412-84-7

www.dolmanscott.co.uk

"touching at fragments of my memory"

the crying shore
melissa maclellan

i dedicate my life to many people.
Some have touched me mentally whilst others have done so physically.
Yet, they all became a part of me
and i thank them for that.

To mum, pops, marlene and patrick
babs and pushkin

Especially for dr. r. mathew

These are the people that believed in me.
That reached out to touch me.
That offered me hope and a destiny.

In the end i created nothing but myself

CONTENTS

SOMETIMES..........................vii

part one
"the first movement of life and disguise"

1

WALKING THROUGH TIME.................2
FLESH OF DREAMS - (1)...............3
THE BOOK OF HURT - Pt 1............10
TO HELL WITH UNCERTAINTY [a].......18
THE BOOK OF HURT - Pt 2............25
MASTER OF GAMES - I................32
FLESH OF DREAMS (2)................39
TO HELL WITH UNCERTAINTY [b].......49
MASTER OF GAMES - II...............57
THE BOOK OF HURT - Pt3.............68
FLESH OF DREAMS (3)................74
FLIGHT OF FANTASY..................81

contents

part two
"passion displays with ice and desire"

83

```
FROM WITHOUT TO WITHIN.............84
TO HELL WITH UNCERAINTY [c].......86
THE MASTER OF GAMES - III.........96
THE BOOK OF HURT - Pt4...........104
FLESH OF DREAMS (4)..............112
THE MASTER OF GAMES - IV.........122
THE BOOK OF HURT - Pt5...........132
TO HELL WITH UNCERTAINTY [d].....139
THE THIRD MOVEMENT OF LIFE AND
  DISGUISE......................144
```

part three
"dancing the dance where fire grows"

147

```
SLICE - MY LIFE..................148
FLESH OF DREAMS (5)..............149
THE BOOK OF HURT - Pt 6..........157
THE MASTER OF GAMES - V..........169
THE BOOK OF HURT - Pt7...........179
THE MASTER OF GAMES - VI.........185
FLESH OF DREAMS (6)..............194
DIRECTION........................204
```

the crying shore

part four
"fluid within tainted rainbows"

205

IMAGES OF BEING	206
TO HELL WITH UNCERTAINTY [e]	207
THE MASTER OF GAMES - VII	216
THE BOOK OF HURT - Pt8	226
FLESH OF DREAMS (7)	235
THE MASTER OF GAMES - VIII	242
THE BOOK OF HURT - Pt9	253
THE MASTER OF GAMES - IX	261
FLESH OF DREAMS (8)	268
THE BOOK OF HURT - Pt10	277
THE MASTER OF GAMES - X	282
THE BOOK OF HURT - Pt11	289
FREAK UNIQUE	291
DAWNING AND MOVING	293

SOMETIMES

sometimes it is the things we do
that create our soul
burns deep into the inside
to hide all our fears
lost like two lovers apart
I swim with uncertainty
into a new world
constructed by men
creating their own Utopia
from within which they can hide
and I am clambering for air
in this world of wasted breath
catching only moments
of a hazy past
and into the red room
I am beckoned to come
releasing broken dreams
entwined with their laughter
I cradle this moment
and allow it to fade
into fantasy and the fantastic
as I shed my skin
onto a dew dropped floor
twisting and turning
gasping for breath
through poisoned skies
I am forced to plunge
star-shaped and proud
awakening a new form
that is covered by sadness
I pierce my soul with moments
and hide the fear

the crying shore

sometimes it is the things we do
that cause the hurt and the pain
as I crawl naked and bare
just to release my anger
I encounter no resistance
just a Utopia
created by men
in which they can hide
and I find nothing
that I can call familiar
except great uncertainty
I find that I am alone
casting outward in whispers
I cry out my sister name
into a pool of crystal
and stare at reflected faces
that are not mine
but now that I am reborn
there can be no more dark places
and as I unfold my wings
to a glistening sun
I await my moment
for I know it will come

part one

"the first movement of life and disguise"

WALKING THROUGH TIME

unfolding time
backwards and through my memories
I am walking on glass
where every fragment causes
pain, blood and tears
creating new darkness
and I want to forget
that you and I ever existed
I want to stop treading
upon these nightmares of mine
to sleep, deep and unmoving
to flow, like a winter's breath
spiralling and upward
and out from the heart
and out from the soul
without consideration
of my placement
my social acting
is distracting, digressing, distressing
causing abstraction
and bi-polarisation
twisting and turning
slowly unwinding
I am walking through time
through all that has been
and seen, deep and unclean
a past that is tainted
yet, pure of heart
I am unfolding time
and walking on glass
waiting for the moment
to slowly pass
I am walking through time
through these memories of mine

FLESH OF DREAMS – (1)

I think that I am now awake. I'm not really that sure when I went to sleep but I feel pain in my head so I guess that I must be awake. There's something else. Something that is making noise on the outside. Not within me but away from me. I can't make it out. I can't see either. All I see is the blackness. There is no colour seeping through. There is only blackness. And this noise. What is it? It's a dull thumping. I've tried to speak to the noise, to plead for it to slow down or shut off but could make no sound, not a sound that I could hear anyway. I wish I knew where I was or how I got here. That's if here is a place. I maybe somewhere else. Heaven crosses my mind for a moment even though I have never believed. I feel as if I am dead but not dead. The noise outside is continuing. Droning in a monotone that makes me think of motor-boat engines. Maybe it is God reaching out to me. I must be dead. If I could remember how I got here then I would know for sure. I try to move but feel as if I have no body. Am I my soul? I try to move again without any success and then stop trying. Something is wrong. I keep telling myself this again and again but I cannot work out what it is. The noise outside stops. I hear only silence. If I am dead and this is my soul then where is God? Where is the bright white light of Heaven's gate that so many have reported awaiting them? Why am I alone? Questions, questions, questions. They flow through me in a torrid fashion as if they were searching for something. All of them interconnected and trying to reach the one answer that would explain what is happening to me. I fall asleep.

The dream feels more real than my reality. I find that I am in a car that is heading south out of a city and towards the open country. The radio is playing a tune that has a constant beat but it is a song that I have never heard. I like it anyhow, and tap my fingers upon the top of the steering wheel as I drive effortlessly down the fast lane at over 100 miles per hour. There is no one else with me in my dream. The car is empty and no cars pass by me, nor do I overtake any one. I am alone. The road lights up in front of me as I drive by the headlights of my car. The outside view is so non-descript that it may all be the same. The car feels real and for a while I wonder if I'd dreamt of Heaven and that this is my reality, or, is it the other way around? I want to stop the car. The feeling of having driven for too long is washing over me and I need to rest. I must have fallen asleep at the wheel momentarily and dreamt of the sensation of Heaven. Sleep would seem to be what I need. To find a hotel and a warm bed for the night before I continue on my journey. But, I have passed nothing on the way that even looked like it might offer me my sanctuary and have seen no signs of anything approaching. I continue, turn up the radio to keep myself awake and wind down the window. The tune continues without a break and I wonder if the station I am tuned to has gone off the air and left the tape playing

part one

for those late night die-hards. Fifty miles pass without contact with anyone or anything. The radio crackles and then finally stops dead and I curse as my hand slaps it, trying desperately to bring it back to life. And then there it is. Neon signed paradise. I touch the brake and bring the car to a slower speed. Up ahead of me a brightly lit forecourt looms. People are climbing in and out of cars and my first signs of life in over a hundred miles makes me feel warm. I pull into the forecourt and stop the car. Across from this tarmac rest-stop is a hotel. Big, bright and welcoming. I have no baggage and so head straight to the hotel's sliding doors. As I approach I nod at several of the people milling around the entrance and smile. I feel tried but polite manners cost nothing and so appear welcoming. As I reach the doors I nod at a person to my left who is smiling at me as if she knows me. Yes, definitely female but do I know her? I smile back and find that this reaction causes her to extend her hand in welcome. She talks but the noise is so loud from the passing cars that I do not hear. Passing cars? I look briefly over my shoulder at the now swarming roadway. A strange panic envelops me for a brief moment as I recall the once empty roadway that had brought me here. The woman is still talking. I tell her that I am looking for a room so that I can get some sleep and this causes her to laugh. The cars die away in the distance.

"Why do you need sleep?" She asks.

"To cure me of this thumping headache and blood-shot eyes. I've been driving for a long while."

"But you are resting already. So why do you need sleep?"

I am confused for a moment. I do not know the answer to her question and yet I feel I owe her some reply. I say nothing instead.

"So. Where are you going to on your journey?" She retorts.

"Going to? I don't know." I feel panic. How could I have been driving? I don't even know where I am driving to or where I have come from.

"I just need to rest." I say. "It's been a long day and I am a little confused."

"There you go again. Why do you need to rest when you are resting already?"

"I don't understand." I reply. "How can I be resting already? I have been driving. I may have rested momentarily as I drove but what I need is long term. A cup of something warm and a place to lay my head. Who are you anyway?"

"I am many different things to many people. Some may say they know me but I believe that only I can know myself."

part one

"Do they call you a name?" I ask. The irrelevance of the question frustrates me. I wonder if I really care for this conversation with a stranger that I'll never meet again.

"Oh! you will see me again." She exclaims. "Now you will always see me. Not just in this place but also in the other places where you shall meet me with confusion. In a way we are now linked. Not by my calling but by yours. You wanted me to be here, beckoned me from afar and now I am here."

She's mad. The poor bitch. The regular nut-case that hassles poor, tired strangers for a few pence to provide her with coffee. Her brain frozen with the cold that envelops the night sky and a lifetime of alcohol. I raise my hand to stop her conversation from going further.

"If you don't mind," I say as politely as possible, "there is a bed in this place with my name on it." I reach into my pocket and withdraw my purse. Unclipping the small change pocket of it I take out some change and hand it to her.

"I'll take your money for now. But I'll always be here with you. Soon you will understand this. "

With this she reaches across and slaps me hard across the face and I scream out as the pain takes hold.

I am awake again. It is still dark and the silence still prevails. I was dreaming again. The same dream every time and every time I wake up I find myself back here. Alone and afraid. I try and remember the last dream I had but can only recall the face of the drunkard old woman outside of the hotel as she cackles and then slaps me. A face that is so clear I can see my own reflection within her brilliant eyes. Is she is right? Will she always be here in some small way. A constant picture within my sub-conscious that replays itself again and again.

The pain in my head is finally lifting. That makes me feel better. I'm not sure how long I have been like this. Trapped in this void but as each moment of time passes I find it harder to retain any form of sanity. It's hard to function normally in a world where there can be only thoughts and dreams. I receive no input from my senses at all. I've tried counting the time away, if only to gain some gauge of my time here, but with my slipping in and out of dreamland have had to abandon any attempt. I know that I am human, or at least I was. I cannot recall my gender, the chronological date or anything else for that matter and yet I retain the ability to have thought. It was this thought that led me to concluded that I was human. I could be wrong however. I could be something else but I can't remember if I was. I feel lost, incomplete somehow, and wish that if death was coming to collect me that it would do so soon. My life is empty - if life is what I feel. Thoughts of Heaven return and I find that they calm

part one

me. Another question enters into my thoughts. How can I know of God? As I attempt to answer this question the noise from the outside returns again in its dull monotone and distracts me for the moment.

THE BOOK OF HURT – Pt 1

October 1999

Thursday **14**

The doctor came around to see me today. Things haven't been going too well since the operation had been performed a few months ago.

"You should take some time out" She had said. "Find a place to retreat to. Somewhere where you can forget about life for a while, relax a little and take stock."

"Fine." I replied. "Like where?"

"Ever thought about going into hospital for a few days?"

"A nut-house you mean?"

"You make it sound like Bedlam", she laughed. "I think that it would do you some good. What harm could it do you? You certainly can't cope here, at home, at the moment. Why not let someone else look after you?"

"And I can leave when I want to?" It was an uneasy suggestion. Even now, as I write it down in this diary, I am wondering if it is the right thing to do. I mean, you hear about such places never letting you out into the real world again, or, at the very least, if they do let you out, then you are left as some drug-crazed zombie for the rest of your life. Still, what option was there?

"They still do electric shock therapy don't they?"

The doctor laughed again. "All you'll be doing is going away for a rest, that's all! No drugs, no shock therapy, just a rest."

I have to admit the offer was tempting. Thirty-three years of my life have gone past, and its fair to say that I've had enough of just surviving. That's how I feel it is, just survival. What sort of life is that and perhaps I needed to break away for a little while. Anyhow, the way I see it, I have little choice. I am pretty-damn close to committing suicide and, despite half wanting to, I also half want to live as well.

"Okay," I'd said. "I'll take your advice and go away for a little while. When do you think they could fit me in?"

"Tonight, if you really wanted too, or tomorrow."

"Tonight is, er, too soon. I'd need to get a few sorted out about the house before I went. Tomorrow sounds better."

"Okay, tomorrow then." She'd got up at this point and concluding the conversation had said, "I'll make all the arrangements and give you a call back a little later tonight."

"Fine," I'd replied, and then rather tentatively said, "I'll look forward to your call."

That was all it took. A suggestion turned into a reality. I must confess that spending any length of time in a nuthouse has been a nightmare of mine for as many years as I can remember. I mean, how do you prove to someone that you are sane when they think that every word you speak contains some form of insanity? Ah well! Its a done deal now. The doctor had call backed, as she promised.

"Its all fixed for tomorrow morning", she'd cheerfully said on the phone around midnight.

"I feel as I am going to an execution and, umh, I am the one being executed"

"Don't worry! These places are okay. The one you are going to has a nice family atmosphere to it. No serious cases, just mild depressives."

"Shit, I suppose that its better than death," I sighed with a hint of desperation. "You'd better give me the details."

"At-a-girl! Okay here they are…"

part one

Now, as the time ticks away, and dawn is slowly rising to mark the day that I enter into the nightmare that has haunted me for as long as I can remember, I find that my thoughts are more tuned to the prospect of killing myself rather than having to endure spending any length of time within a psychiatric ward at the local hospital. We all have our own images of such places, what they are like and what they contain, and mine are projections of Victorian Sanatoriums in which visitors came and gazed with wonder at the lunatics paraded about before them. No longer would I be one of the gazers, so to speak, but I was to become one the gazed upon. I feel uneasy about this. For years I have been a control freak, even down to the minor details in my life, and now I am about relinquish that control to another person. I'd heard the stories, who hadn't, about not being able to get back out again or about the type of people that were institutionalised. People get hurt in such places. Violence is part of life in psychiatric wards, isn't it? I guess I'll find out for myself in ten hours or so.

Right now, at this very moment, I am lying in my bed thinking. Just thinking and writing. My world has been turned upside down. A few months ago I would have laughed at the suggestion that I take some time out.

"Too busy," I would have said.

That was a few months ago. Then I had been relatively successful. My life had been one of contentment. I was on the up, as they say, the future was bright and a pathway had been laid for me to walk. I'm an academic by trade, writing my Ph.D. and writing various papers for publication within numerous journals. I was also attending, or due to attend, various conferences. Not a bad lot for someone so new to the game of academia. People are, seemingly, impressed by my contributions and this, in turn, fuels me even more. I am over worked and stressed for sure, but who isn't in this day and age? Anyhow, I have to work hard for good lecturing positions are hard to come by at present.

Amazing what a few months can do for you. I'd had an operation four or five weeks ago, a rather serious piece of surgery, and this, I think, has taken its toll upon my well being. Certainly, from that point up to now I seem to have been loosing the plot bit by bit and day by day. I had attempted suicide the day after being released from the hospital but a friend had found me before I'd had the chance to take any quantity of pills and, after a visit to the doctor, that had been the end of that. Yet, it wasn't - the end I mean. The thought remained locked within my head. Eating away with each day. My doctor had prescribed anti-depressants and sedatives but they didn't stop the thoughts, merely stopped me from being bothered to do anything about it. I still cried, still do and am doing so at this moment. Yet, I cry not so much in

part one

desperation but due to the fact that I have wasted my life. A contradiction to what I have said previously perhaps? Not really. Social and personal success are two different things in my book. What is a success to some is a failure for others.

Now I am at this point in my life. Waiting for the time when I will carted off to the nut-house. Strange days indeed. Days that I am unused to. Days that have no meaning, just an existence. I must confess, that I rather like this way of living. It has a warmth to it. A comfort that I have never know before. Not living - just breathing. Thoughts come and go through my head without any secondary considerations. I can think without thinking. Existence. The one thought that remains a constant is that of my death. It is something that I have planned down to the finest detail. In a weird way it is the one motivation that makes me continue to use life. A Paradox. I must use life to find death. I have so much to do before I die, a control freak to the end, and when that is achieved I will terminate my life upon this planet forever. Not a depressing thought, not to me, but one that is needed and necessary. As I said, it drives me to and through life.

The phone has just rung beside my bedside. It was my doctor again. The time is 7.30 in the morning and I haven't slept at all. She was just checking up, asking if everything was all right. I think she had an ulterior motive. The conversation went like this.

"Hi Melissa!"

"Oh, hi. Anything wrong?"

"No, no." I'd heard her shuffling some papers. "I was just checking that you were still going ahead with what we agreed."

"As you've already said," I'd sighed, "what choice do I have? I've got nothing left to loose", I continued.

"Good girl! Do you want me to drive you or can you make your own way there?"

"Nah, its okay. I can find my own way thanks."

"If you're sure?" I'm getting a strange feeling that she is desperate to send me off on my way. If I'd been sailing off into the sunset I'm sure, by her enthusiasm, that she would have been at the quay side waving her white handkerchief, tears in her eyes.

"Its nice to know you care." I said without her detecting my slight undertone of sarcasm.

So, my bags are packed, my life is a mess and I am about to nail the lid of my coffin by living out my worse fear. Who said life couldn't get any worse? Hopefully, I'll be pleasantly surprised and totally wrong by the whole

part one

experience but I don't so. Logically, or as logically as it gets for me, I know that I will soon be entering into a pit of hell. That once I am part of the great psychiatric machine I will be spat at and out without any control over what I can do. My life is in their hands. I just prey that they are safe hands.

TO HELL WITH UNCERTAINTY [a]

Beating bones and carving flesh. His body was racked with a pain. Tiny droplets of blood pulsed through openings across his back. He smiled as the pain hit him again. Watching himself in the mirror that had been placed in front of himself he saw the pleasure upon his face. Via a second mirror, placed behind his body, he viewed the tiger-striped lines that ran across his buttocks and torso. He smiled again, watching with a glee that few would understand. He was kneeling upon the floor. His head and body pushed slightly forward to allow him to observe what was going on behind and forcing his buttocks to protrude behind him. A purposeful protrusion that allowed the whip to make maximum contact and to cause the most pain as it bore down again upon his body. His gaze never left the mirror. His concentration no longer focused upon this world but upon the world that was reflected to him. The world of domination.

Yet, this was no ordinary domination. This was masturbatory domination. A self inflicted domination that involved no second party. Between his thighs his right hand was clasped upon his penis, pumping it frantically and pulling the foreskin back and forth across the head. His left hand held the riding whip that had already left its mark this night. Yet, this was not some uncontrollable, manic thrashing but precisely placed smacks. He drew his left arm up again and brought it back down across the middle of his back with full force.

"Ah!" The first wave of pain hit him. "Shit!"

The second wave brought the pleasure back and he smiled at himself again. His gaze fell upon the reflection of his beaten back. He ran the whip gently up and down. Drawing the tip of it through the lines of blood and spreading it thinly and evenly.

"You sick bastard. You fucking sick bastard," He sneered still pumping at his penis. "You filthy, sick and disgusting bastard."

He beat himself again. The phone ran and it distracted from his reflective world for a brief moment. A tiny moment that forced him to stop the masturbating and the beating and to see himself as he really was. Alone and afraid. It was only a moment and then it was gone. Yet, this fleeting time gave him not so much a regret but a greater determination. The controllable smacks suddenly became more frantic and less placed as the ringing of the phone faded and his reflective world sucked him back into itself again.

"I hate you!" He screamed at the reflection. "I fucking hate you! Everything I fucking do is controlled by you. You! You sick fucker. You fucked-up little shit. You disgust me."

He whipped himself a dozen or so more times and then dropped the whip. He brought his left hand through his buttocks and grabbed at his testicles. His right hand was still working upon himself. His left hand gently cupped his testicles for a few moments before he began to close his fist, encasing his balls tighter.

"I'm gonna rip off your balls you filthy pervert. I'm gonna tear them from your body and stuff them up your arse and then I'm gonna watch you bleed." There was a manic undertone to his voice. He was close to ejaculating but he tried to hold it back. "I'm gonna stuff your balls up your arse and drink your spunk."

He squeezed his testicles as hard as he could. The pain was intense. He felt himself blacking out for a moment from the agony but it did not deter him. He squeezed a second time and felt the testicles flatten and elongate before releasing the grip totally and allowing his hand to slide from his testicles to his anus. Two fingers slipped in. He pushed them into his anus, up to the knuckle. Once placed he pulled his two fingers apart, to form a 'V'-shape, and began to finger his arse.

"Ah! God! I'm gonna cum! No! No! Not yet!" He relaxed his right hand movement and slowed down the pace of both hands until they were moving to an equal rhythm. The gaze was smiling back at him. In this context it was a face he recognised but he had video taped himself once.

part one

Video taped a similar masturbatory experience that he had later played back. He had hated it. It was not the him that he recognised but another him. It had looked sick and vile and had the images had disturbed him for a number of months, causing him to stop the beatings and the self inflicted pain through disgust and embarrassment at what he had observed upon the tape.

He lay upon his back, his legs spread apart. His right hand was still placed around his penis, beating out the same rhythm but his left hand had departed from playing with his anus and began to lick at the two fingers that had been placed within his anus. He licked at them for mere seconds before allowing them to slip into his mouth whereby he began to suck desperately. Inside his mouth he worked his tongue around the two fingers, licking at every area encountered. He tasted himself. Sucked and swallowed and masturbated. He drew his legs together as he did so and, in one movement, rocked himself backwards, forcing his legs up over his head. He could still see in the mirrors. Was still lost in the reflective world of the other him. He could see his body, red and beaten, with its arse in the air and his knees now placed at either side of his head, spine curved to its greatest extent. Above his face now hung his penis, four or five inches away, his right hand still clasped at it, pumping. His two fingers slipped from his mouth.

He used this free hand to locate the riding whip again. He gently beat his back several times in order to get use to the unusual whipping angle before bringing it down harder upon his buttocks. His gaze still remained focused upon the mirrors reflection. He repeated the action several times.

"This is what you deserve, you fucker. You don't deserve anything better, do you?" It was a question he often asked himself, even when not masturbating. "You little shit are just getting what you deserve. I'm gonna take you to an inch of your life, you fucking pervert."

He let the control slip again and began to increase the velocity of the beatings. Now reaching the point of ejaculation he felt uncontrollable and desperate to the point of no longer feeling the manic thrashing that was being inflicted upon himself. His right hand increased in speed also, reading the rhythms of the whip and following their flow. Beating at his flesh with both hands maniacally he felt himself reaching the point of orgasm.

"Come on. Come on. I want to drink you." He pleaded to his hovering penis. "I want to die, tasting you." He opened his mouth expectantly, ready to catch his own semen.

"Come on, you bastard. Let me taste how disgusting and vile you are, you sick fucker." His body spasmed and his rhythms increased. He felt himself blacking out again but fought to remain conscious for these few final moments.

part one

Then it happened. One final spasm and, whilst still peering into the mirrors, allowed his penis to release its semen in to his mouth. He continued to masturbate. causing some of the orgasm to miss his mouth and splatter upon his lips, his eyes and his cheeks. He licked at his lips. His left hand slowed its pace as the intensity of the orgasm began to die away. He allowed his legs to drop back upon the floor. It was over.

Wiping his face with the back of his right hand. he sat up and stared into the mirror. The reflection was slowly becoming the stranger again. The strange being that disgusted him but it was a slow process of change. He brought his knees together again and his arms across them. Placing his jaw upon his folded arms, he stared deeper into the mirror.

"Who are you?" Was all he asked. Then he spoke it only within his head. He repeated the statement again and again within himself before, expelling a long and deep sigh, he repeated himself out aloud to the reflection. "Who the fuck are you? What are you?" The reflection said nothing back but deep within himself he knew that the person being reflected back was himself. Nothing more than that. Not another being but a different part of himself. The sexual self perhaps but he had never really thought that deeply about it. He sighed again.

"I just want to know what the fuck is going on! What the hell is happening to me?" He felt sick from the taste of his semen and lost his chain of thought of a minute as he considered vomiting. "Who are you?" he repeated for the last time.

Looking into the mirrors he cast his eyes onto his back. Looked at the lines of red and at the blood that was still creeping from the wounds. His back hurt. He felt sure that he would not be able to sit properly for a couple of days and then felt sick again. This time it was not the semen but his reflected self that made him want to be sick.

"I hate you," was all he said.

Then he began to cry.

THE BOOK OF HURT – Pt 2

October 1999

Friday **15**

As I write this diary entry I am sitting amidst the 'nice family atmosphere' that my doctor had promised existed within this ward. Perhaps it does, but if it does it is more akin to the Adam's Family than my own. Its a weird place filled to bursting with even weirder people. Then, what should one expect from such a place? My resting period will not, I think, be an easy thing to achieve. Six hours here already and I can feel the stress mounting within my bones. I've been housed with the men,

"Just for the time being," she had said. I'm just not quite sure what it is all about at the moment. What do people do here? No doubt that luxury will become apparent to me with time. Time again. Already it has become an obsession to me. Tick-tock-tick, grand father time and the hourglass sand drip slowly through these words and into my life. Six hours and I feel as if I am going mad already!

My bedroom, that is what they are called here, is more like a cell within a minimum security prison. The door contains a window whose eye never sleeps and, opposite the doorway, a large panelled window that is both constructed of toughened glass and unable to open any more than a few inches allows some light to filter into this artificial reality. As you walk into the room, on the left hand side, is the bed, complete with reading light, and a wardrobe without any hangers.

"In case you use them to harm yourself," she had said. On the other side of the wall is a wash basin, a chair and a chest of drawers. Descriptions are not needed. Image any hospital within this great isle of ours and you can picture these items. The walls are green and bordered with a flower pattern.

"Make yourself at home," She'd said. I wasn't quite sure if she was hiding a smile or not. I certainly wasn't. I was in fear. 'She', by the way, was my assigned nurse. The person that I went to when I needed to know. The person that, already I was sure, would be watching me and my movements. Reporting me to a file that housed other pieces of information about myself and my doings. She has a name, but that is not important now. She is the enemy.

"We don't like to see our relationship with the patients as a 'us' and 'them' thing," she'd said. "If you need to talk just ask one of the staff and they will talk to you." So, what do you do, I am left wondering? Can't I talk to you? I didn't follow up this puzzle. A friend of mine works in psychiatric wards and she had filled me in about what was what and how things functioned. I know that her job, in reality, is to try and avoid me as much as possible. I get the feeling, with this particular nurse, that business is business and that things have a particular time and place. She looks efficient. Out of place in here and more suited to an office environment. She looks bitchy, but that could just be me. Paranoid already! Wow, this place grips you at the throat with no relenting.

"Everything you need to know is in this blue booklet. Who your consultant is, your ward doctor, times of stuff, etc., etc."

"Consultant? Ward doctor? What are they?" Ah! the bliss of child-like ignorance.

She'd sighed. Deeply I remember thinking, perhaps too deeply. As if it were all simple really. As if I should be an old hand at this by now. "Your consultant deals with the drugs and over-sees your care plan, the ward doctor examines you in greater detail."

"Drugs? Examine?" My questions were, at this point, flowing frantically, even if lacking in any great depth. " I don't want drugs!"

"We'll see what the consultant says." Smiled knowingly. "Now if there is anything else you want to know? Oh yeah, I'll be back in a few minutes to show you where everything is. Okay?"

"Ah! yeah. Okay." I had tried to sound braver than I felt.

"Make yourself at home." If this had been my home I would have moved a long time ago. So, whilst waiting, I'd unpacked my few things. Wash stuff by the wash basin, clothes thrown on the wardrobe floor due to lack of hangers and music and books by the bedside. Then what? Minutes turned into half an hour, then an hour, then I began to panic. I'd looked out of my cell-door window at the empty, artificially lit corridor but saw, nor heard, nothing. Where had she gone. Was I forgotten? I remembered that soap series 'The Prisoner' and I'd began, to myself of course, to chant "I am not a number but a human being." Fat lot of good it did for me.

Six hours and she still hadn't returned. Night was beginning to close and, after reading the blue book that seemed to promise a lot more than what was really on offer, was beginning to crave a cigarette or three, for that matter. Hence, my writing this. I'm too scared to go outside this door and no one seems to be coming in. I occasionally look out of the toughened glass window at the benches sitting upon the paving slabbed entrance but then remember that the ward entrance door was locked on my way in. To keep 'them' out or 'us' in? 'Us' in, I have no doubt. Within that six hour wait I had heard noise eventually. Next door to me in fact. Talking, I think it was, but it sounding like someone babbling. It lasted for a few hours and scared me shitless whatever it was. This was the shape of things

part one

to come. Strange people with drugged minds. We've all seen 'One Flew Over The Cuckoo's Nest", laughed at its portrayals, but here it was, in the flesh, awaiting me. Daring me to exit my cell-like womb into an uncharted world. No! Worse than that. An uncharted and monster infested world where dinosaurs with big teeth still lurked and people shrunk heads for fun. Even worse, it begun but a few inches through either wall.

I also have the strange feeling that my doctor has lied somewhat to me. The impression that I have already is that, if they see fit to do so, my free will can be removed by these people called 'nurses'. 'How' and 'why' are mysterious questions that I'm sure will eventually receive an answer in some shape or form. All I know is what my little blue bible tells me. I think I'll read it again later just to fill myself in on a few finer details.

My brain is screaming for a cigarette. The outside is getting darker now. Six and a half hours have gone by. I know that you can smoke in here, the bible tells me so, but I bet that everyone in this place smoke like chimneys. What else is there to do? I could go and look for the rooms where you can smoke but everytime I gain the courage to place my hand upon the door handle someone does something that, outside of this context, would be deemed a little strange and I return to my gazing or my bed. I could sleep for a while but then what do you do when night time comes? What time do we have to go to bed? Do we have to go to bed at all? I need a cigarette. I've got to go outside. Got to face this world inhabited by aliens and loonies.

I saw my chance a little later after writing those previous paragraphs. A fat moustachioed man had entered my room, just as I was reaching my point of despair. The blue bible had let me down again by proving itself lacking in informing me of the precise time that the main doors were locked. I was in need of both cigarettes and someone to notice I was still here and alive. The fat man gave me the opportunity to quench all these things.

"Want some food?" He'd causally said through a half-opened doorway.

"Nah! Thanks anyway. I'm not really hungry." Seizing my chance, and without pausing for any breath, had added, "can I go for a cigarette?" rapidly followed by "and what time do the doors to the outside close?"

"You sure you don't want food?" Dumb fuck. What about my questions? He seems to be a very strange individual, in my opinion. Maybe he use to be an ex-patient. Why knows? You hear it all the time in the social care world don't you? Ex- junkie running a drug program. Ex- car thief showing the police how they do it. Ex- nutter working at the local nut-house. Maybe that is him. He certainly looks the part. Not that he looks mad or anything its just that he has a weird expression that more often than not crosses his face. Sort of lost and bewildered.

Anyhow the questions had been answered after his ignorant reply. I'd got my half an hour of nicotine freedom. I even managed to cram in three cigarettes before the locks were turned that would seal me in here for the night. The doors are locked at eight to eight-thirty, by the way, for future reference. Now, I am back in my room. Sitting in various places, trying to find the one that best fits what I am looking for in a sitting position. I chose the floor, in the end, placing myself under the window, between the sink and the wardrobe, back pressed against the radiator. Its not that its cold in here but more a case of my being able to gain maximum visibility from this position. I'm not sure what happens next. A cup of tea would be nice, and a little joint, but I don't know. I've been left alone in this place again. After the fat man came to ask about supper only one other person has shown their face around my door and that was only to ask,

"You all right?" and then he was gone. Door closed, observation window opened. As soon as he had left I'd close the observation window from the inside. They could still see, if they wanted to, but they had to want to see. A mere glance would show them nothing. I must confess that I am a little afraid of this place. I feel as if I want to cry but I'm too scared to in case someone hears me. I hope tomorrow is better than this!

MASTER OF GAMES – I

Devious was certainly a word that could be applied to Andrew. Indeed, he had often used the term to describe himself and did so with a sense of pride. He preferred to call himself a mind player, a manipulator of other's thoughts, but devious was equally as fitting given the circumstances. He considered himself to be good at it. None of his large circle of friends was aware of his ability to get them to do things for him and certainly none suspected that Andrew often played one friend against the other in order to reach the top of their social ladder. Evil perhaps, but there was a skill involved in this gamesmanship that required many hours of fine tuning and the ability to maintain such deception was an art that was, to Andrew at least, second to none. He'd had to loose several people, cannon-fodder as he called them, along the way but then new friends were so easy to make in the small town. Currently, his scheming was running at over-drive. Sex was one of those things that seemed to drive most men and for Andrew it was something that was central to the majority of his games. One of the games he was playing right now involved it. Like a finely-honed machine his brain was twisting people to suit his desire. It was not always easy. Sometimes he would reach a dead-end situation and have to back-track to a new starting point but he didn't play with speed. He could take his time and wait for it to happen knowing that the event would come eventually. It always did.

part one

Mike had been like a brother to Andrew for as long as both of them could remember. They had shared in each other's bad times and partied with the good days. Mike had been a pawn but only when it was really necessary for the game to be so. Most of the time he was left alone. Perhaps a true friend, perhaps not, Andrew had never really given it that much thought. But faithful to each other they were. Their lives were very similar. Both were currently spending a period of leisure time at Social Security's expense, had long standing girlfriends who adored them and a social life that would make many envious. They may have had it all. But all was what Andrew wanted. A taste of every little bit of life was desired and needed to satisfy himself properly. This was his mission.

The pub that they were both sitting in held little attraction. Its saving grace was the fact that both of their girlfriends worked there. Apart from that, the occasional free drink and cheap food there was nothing of notable substance to draw them in. It was spring, summer was fast approaching you could feel it on the wind, and the day was pleasant enough to be able to spend a few afternoon hours just sitting around and talking. It was a good day to be unemployed.

" Seeing Jenny tonight then ?" Mike queried as he looked towards the bar.

"Shush! For god's sake keep it down will you. Do you want Donna to find out?"

"I don't care either way. It's not really my problem is it?" He drew upon a cigarette. "Anyhow, you haven't mentioned her in ages. Are you two still seeing each other behind Donna's back?"

"Well," Andrew paused to take a drink. "Things are getting a bit weird at the moment. I spoke to her last night and she dropped a bombshell that you are just not going to believe!"

Andrew stopped talking. Pause within conversation was a good effect and he knew how to use it effectively. He took another drink and casually looked around the bar. Two people were playing Pool just behind Mike and as he continued his gaze he caught sight of Claire, Mike's girlfriend, behind the bar who was stacking glasses upon the shelves. He considered her for a moment. She was not really a beautiful looking woman and yet there was something attractive about her. He had thought about her before, sometimes whilst masturbating, but her relationship with Mike seemed too strong for her to play around with other men. Andrew looked away, continuing his perusal of the bar area. There was a couple sitting near the doorway, on the right, with their backs faced towards the wall.

part one

"She thinks that she might be pregnant." Andrew let the last word roll off his tongue slowly just to make sure it registered itself within his companions brain. "She's got a doctor's appointment tomorrow morning at the Health Clinic."

"Wow! What you gonna do?"

"Leave the country," Andrew said with a slight laugh.

"No, seriously?" Mike edged forward upon his chair and rested one arm upon the table to support his head. "If she is pregnant you know that you are going to have to tell Donna. Jesus!" He sat back again as he said it. " I surely wouldn't like to be in your shoes at the moment. When Donna finds out she is going to hit the roof."

"Tell me about it. It's not as if I really like Jenny or anything."

He sounded callous, but then, how he sounded and how he thought were rarely entwined and the same. His callousness was wholly due to the fact that Jenny was not the game. She was a pawn, ready to be taken from the game. If honesty were traded here, and it wasn't often, then it would be a true statement to say that Jenny was not even living flesh and bone. She resided within Andrew's imagination. Conjured up purely because such a person was necessary for the game to succeed. She provided camouflage, created distraction from the real purpose of the game.

"Anyhow," Andrew said, "what's happening between you and Claire?" He shot Claire a quick glance but she didn't notice.

Mike plucked up his half empty pint glass, but did not make any drinking motion with it; merely held it.

"Same as before, you know?" He drew the glass to his lips and allowed a little to trickle into his mouth. "I don't know! She just doesn't seem interested in me anymore. What do you think? Is she having an affair or not? Peter reckons that she is but, well, I don't know"

"Look Mike," Andrew reached a hand across the circular table and placed it upon Mike's forearm, squeezing it slightly. "You and I both know that Claire loves you, Right? We also know that Peter fancies her like crazy, Okay? So, lets just say that he has an ulterior motive for saying the things he does. Why don't you just speak to her?"

Mike shrugged. That pathetic, lost-boy shrug that he always gave when in defeat. It annoyed the hell out of Andrew. Always had done. The shrug, the 'help-me' face, sad and lonely.

part one

"Okay! You want my opinion? Claire loves you, even I can see that. As for the sex? Well, I don't know but, and if you want me to be honest, I'd say that you should stop playing the 'happy hippie' and show her a more passionate side. You know? Take her out, give her something else to talk about apart from guitar scales, music or your family crisis."

"Yeah, like where?" Mike gulped another mouthful of his beer.

"What about a film? Some dinner? Come on man use your imagination, you know what she likes."

"She talks to you better," Mike replied, perhaps with a hint of jealousy. He stood up, finished the last of his drink and, grabbing the empty glass in front of Andrew, headed for the bar.

"Oh! I know what Claire wants," Andrew said to no one in particular. "I know better than she does. Only she doesn't realise it yet, but she will. Time is what I have to play with."

Andrew glanced at the bar. Mike stood in front of it, head propped by one arm, talking to the manager and pointing to the spirit prices with his free hand. Claire was pouring the drinks, seemingly uninterested in their conversation. When the first glass was filled, she lifted it up onto the bar top and upon the awaiting drip-tray. Picking up the second glass in her left hand, she placed the right upon the pump and, as she did so, glanced across at Andrew and similed. Nothing else just a smile. To Andrew, the smile said it all. It was a smile that suggested a future, a need to talk. A smile that hinted at a deeper lurking unhappiness. A smile that he knew he could break through.

"My dear Watson, " Andrew whispered, "the game, it seems, is afoot, " and having said it laughed out aloud for all to hear and, momentarily, causing the pool players to stop and look over.

FLESH OF DREAMS (2)

The droning noise did something strange. It called a name. Not just a drone, as per normal, but something, a name, that was crystal clear. I can't remember what the name was, of course, that would be too easy. Yet, it was there. The first time caught me by surprise. It was wedged in between a long drone and three shorter, quicker ones. I wasn't ready for it, I was back thinking about god, only half aware. I waited an age for a second mention but it never came and, as a consequence forgot about the name. I am still not sure what noises or gestures I can achieve though but I try to shout to establish contact. I just hope that I made a connection. There was no further attempt at the name again though and can only conclude that my returns went unnoticed. As I've said before, I'm not sure 'who' or 'what' I am. My brain was seemingly trying to make contact with mouth, arms and legs but I'm really not all that sure I have any. When I dream, I dream that I am human but, then we all dream strange things don't we?

Still, progress is at least being made. The droning noise can speak a language that I understand although, it seems to prefer not to. As for the 'who's' and the 'what's' of it all I am, I must admit, still in defeat. Ninety-ish percent of me now says human but as to what is wrong with me is unanswerable and a constantly circular question. At least time is still working and, therefore, hopefully the future will shed a little more light upon this. I've certainly gone away from the idea of being dead or waiting for god and heaven. Its not really something I understand a great deal about anyway, I am not very clear-cut in my religious beliefs.

Some things are becoming clearly however. For one, I know what such words such as 'god' mean to me. I have thought, the ability to rationalise and a vocabulary. I also dream, or at least I believe I do, even if it is always the same dream and even if I never remember beyond a slap. The last couple of times, in the dream, I have tried to catch glimpses of myself within her eyes. Just to see how I dream myself looking, but of course, when I peer deeply I become lost in her eyes and cannot find my way out again until she slaps me across the face. Neither can I picture her. I can't explain it. I see her in totality, so complete and alive, but when I focus upon any particular aspect of her being it seems to dissolve into a whiteness as if someone were removing the paint from this picture.

I wonder if that name, it was definitely a name and not just a word, I wonder if it could have been my name? Christ I wish I had remembered it. It sounded so warm and comforting, like a return home, back to some physical reality. I'm sure I saw mental images flash through me when it was mentioned. Were they pictures of me? Fragments, perhaps, of my past? Did these images even

part one

contain people? I can't recall anymore but I think, just to be on the safe side, I'll keep one 'ear cocked', so to speak, just in case it should happen again. This time though I'll be prepared for it. I'll store the name and capture the images with as much clarity as I can muster. Next time I'll be waiting, that's for sure, next time.

The constant dream I have been having has begun to shift. Its is no longer static but progressive. It moves along, quickly filling in those parts already experienced, as if to refresh me in some way. Which, given my memory, is a welcomed event.

The radio plays, the car pushes, no, rather it glides, forward. I remain alone. I see the rest-stop, pull in and get out. I see the same people outside, make the same gestures. All remains the same. The only changing factor is that this time the woman is not at the doorway to greet me. There is a space, a void, where she stood before which causes me to stop and look around for a few moments. I'm unsure if I am looking for her or just seizing the moment to absorb my surroundings. As I look around, I realise that everything is as it always is. I turn full circle, slowly, and stop dead as the two giant, grass-green and panelled doorways welcome me with an automatic opening and a quiet 'Hush'. The first thing to hit me is the smell. Not unpleasant, quite the opposite, a warm smell that reminds me of bed, coffee, iced doughnuts and every other wondrous thing to have entered my life.

I pause, unclip my shoulder bag, reach in for a packet of cigarettes, slide one out of the packet and the bag and bring it to my lips. I return for the lighter, close the bag and reposition it upon my left shoulder, cough gently, touch at my hair with my free hand and pass underneath the impressive hotel entrance.

The inside equals the doors and their frames. The smell remains enticing. Aromatic yet, not over powering. I light the cigarette and move two paces forward. Directly in front of me, centrally placed, a wooden crescent shaped reception desk radiates. The entire lighting system within the foyer area seems set up to focus and move you towards it. I resist it for a minute, still absorbing the aroma, the impressive desk area, drawing upon my cigarette. To the left and right of the desk are two lounge areas with crystal white sofas and wooden coffee tables. People are sitting upon them here and there but my concentration upon the lounge serves merely as a lead. A lead that takes me away from these areas and onto the double staircases that spin upwards besides the almighty welcome desk. These, in turn, lead me back to this desk. Above the desk in passive neon, the stylised name of the hotel is illuminated. It reads "The Shore Hotel".

I walk down the welcome carpet, smoking the last few millimetres of tobacco and chemicals and, without even acknowledging a need for one, an ashtray is presented to me by the arm of a bell boy. I extinguish

part one

the cigarette and smile at the efficiency, pleasantly pleased. A few more steps and I am up against the monolithic wooden slab.

"Welcome to The Shore. A room?" the counter clerk enquired, already turning away to collect a key off the rack behind him.

"Yeah, er, sure, I guess."

He turns back and offers a key with his outstretched hand. It reads '00010110'. I conclude straight away that it is in binary but I can not understand it. I hesitate to ask and, fortunately, am interrupted before my jaw drops.

"Anything wrong?" The clerk enquires puzzled. "this room is one of the best in the hotel. A change perhaps?"

"No. no. Its fine." I take a step backwards and look at the two staircases leading off into opposing ends of the hotel. The signs offer no hope as everything is in binary, I stand still confused.

"Are you all right?" The clerk asks.

"Ah, I'm not sure. Is there a porter?"

"Yes, certainly," he replies as his hand quickly pushes down upon a bell and, gaining someone's attention, begins to wriggle his forefinger in a 'come here' gesture. The boy who donated the ashtray appears by my side.

"Room 00010110, Tiko," he gestures to the left staircase, "No baggage."

I follow up the staircase and down two corridors before stopping at a door. Tiko inserts the key and we enter into the room. I unclipped my bag again, removing my purse and began to draw out some money as a tip.

"No, no, its fine. No tipping required", she said.

For the first time I noticed the gender of the bell person. A closer inspection revealed that not only was this a woman but it was the same woman that had slapped my face time and time again.

"So, Tiko is your name?" I sat upon the bed. "That was you outside, before, wasn't it?"

"It was," she announced. "But Tiko is just a name for some. As I have said to you, people know me by many different names, names that will grow with time, but only I know myself."

"So you work here?"

part one

"Here and there. I find myself in many places and known as many things."

"But why do you slap me?"

"This place, here," she out stretched her arms, "is a place for journey people. People who seek. It is a temporary place, a place of transition. It is not where you should lie forever. Living in this place, this space, is a need not a desire. Before long you will see this to be true. Now you have made it. Entered into the 'Shore Hotel' and began a process. It is a process that I, amongst others, will guide you through but be warned, some you can trust, others you can not. Just remember not to dwell here. Do not wish it. That is my job to make sure that this will not happen."

"But, this is just a dream, right?" I say. "I can wake up when I want to or when I need to, right?"

"You're not listening are you? This dream is the dream of 'The Shore. You brought yourself here but, I stress again, only I can remove you from it. Without me you will be here for a long time. You have to trust me. You should have trusted me outside all those times but you didn't. You couldn't anyhow, only passion and desire open the entrance doors and your search for me outside of the dream context showed that you felt these things. Anyhow, here we both are and, after that speech, any questions at all?"

"I want to leave."

"You can not."

"I wish you would go."

"I can not."

"I wish you would stop hurting me."

"I can not."

I wish you would show me beautiful things."

"Ah! That I can do. Close your eyes." I closed them. "Think of yourself for a while. Can you see beauty?"

"I can't," I complained.

"Look deeper."

"I can't. I'm just thinking about you. About what you said."

"Then you are not quite ready. Take this in your left hand." She pushed something spherical into the palm. "It may help, it may not. It will help only if you never truly see its depth. If you do, however The Shore hotel will remove all your privileges and banish you back to square one. Are you holding it tightly?"

part one

"Yes," I replied.

"Ah! Good. Now don't drop it," and with that she slapped me across the face once again and it all vanished.

I awoke with the image of the sphere. It looked like a map of the world, only different countries, places that I fail to recognise. What was it she'd said. Not to look too deep into its depths. But how deep is that? How can I understand this image if I fear to look at it! What will it tell me? Do I need to decipher its meaning before I can progress? Can I afford to look at all? Maybe just carrying it with me mentally is all I need to do for now. What if.....?

I hear the name again! Wait! Damn these dreams for their distraction. What name was it? This time I felt the images but failed to see. This name is the key to unlocking where, who or what I am. Damn! Even after I promised my self that I would be more vigilant. Now the name has gone through me again, with its information and pictures. I think about the sphere again. Is there a connection between the object and the name. I can't help but wonder if all this is a game where I am merely an active piece rather than the core of it.

The drone has ceased yet again and I can continue my thoughts without distraction for a while and try to create a more coherent feel to all this. Tentatively, I reopen the spherical image and begin to focus upon other layers.

Then, scared by the constant warnings that whiz through my thoughts decide to be slightly more delicate in my methods. I retreated back to the question of looking at the connection between sphere, the name and myself. Not to mentioned the still unanswered questions, and there were still plenty of those!

TO HELL WITH UNCERTAINTY [b]

They were at a party. Him, her and a face that was recognisable to him but only within another context. Alcohol and numerous other drugs had beaten them to the doorway but were as equally welcoming as they were wanted by the three. If the drugs objected to their treatment, they did so quietly. Cannabis, speed and LSD flowed easy. These were the days before the big 'E', before the throbbing hordes of electro-repetitive junkies, it was a time of music, some dancing, but mainly it was about sex. That was brought what them here and that was what carried him also. He was no different in that respect. As each drug held itself in place within his system he slowly began to switch off his mind and allow his body to flow with its own desires and needs. Searching out the crowds with its prime directive firmly encoded.

His girlfriend, 'her', was sitting in a corner of the main dance room, rolling a joint, whilst astride a brown bean bag. The other girl, 'she' from a different context, had her body upon the carpeted floor, legs folded underneath her and her head listed sideways upon the girlfriend's lap. He approached them and sat down in front of them with a drug induced smile slicing across his face.

"You girls having fun?" He mouthed.

"Be better if you were here," The girl from another context said.

"Well, I'm here now. Why don't we go somewhere a little more private?" He cruised the room with his eyes. "Fancy going upstairs?"

"Yeah, once the joint is rolled," the girlfriend slurred.

"Mind if I come?" Interjected context girl.

"More the merrier! Sounds like fun. I'll go and locate us some quite space."

Then he was gone. Entering into the black sea of sweating, swaying bodies without even a backward glance. A mission imprinted upon his hard-wiring and a will, if not a desperation, to succeed.

Time passed. The joint was roach upon his return but he toked upon it anyway and then stubbed it.

"Roll another one?" She enquired.

"Wait till we get there," he said, "there's plenty of time for that. Just follow me to your land of dreams and ecstasy." He laughed at the image, then stood up and offered a hand to each female. They both accepted and he drew them to their feet.

part one

"Keep a hold! I don't want to loose anyone," he shouted as they entered the swarm, carving their way through towards the room's exit which they located without a hitch.

"Just the stairs and then...."

"Climbing our way to Nirvana," context girl giggled.

"All aboard the ship of fools"

"Fools that fool around," his girlfriend said before staggering up the first few steps and, gripping the banister said, "Which way to paradise?"

The room which he had located was sparsely lit but it held a double mattress upon the floor. Surrounding it were crumpled clothes, a few records and a week of living. Plates mounted the surface area that had been originally designed for work but it was all minor stuff. It was the double mattress that loomed and shone out at them.

"Three-two-one!" They rushed up to and dived upon the soft foam laughing. Thrashing their arms and legs as they reached ground zero.

"Let the games begin," he was excited.

"I'll roll the joint."

"Who wants one of these?" Context girl said producing a bag of trips from her jacket pocket. She handed one to each of them and took one for herself.

"Who wants one of these?" He said, undoing the button fly to his jeans and releasing his erect penis.

"Ummh!" Both girls said in unison and then, looking at one another, the girlfriend said, "you first, I'll roll the joint."

Three naked bodies, Marking each other with bites, kisses, scratches and fluids. He lay upon his back, legs slightly apart, whilst his girlfriend slid her 'O' shaped mouth over and down the length of his penis. Her name was Jen. The girl from the different context was called Lorna, a girl he had met within a similar scene a hazy past ago. Jen took him to his length, her tongue flicked at the moistened head, working its way around and up, until it sought the eye of the penis. Once located, she inserted the tip of her tongue to its furthest point. He arched his back, trying to extend his final few inches into her mouth, but this was her game. She tilted her head backwards, denying him his pleasure and made laughing noises that concluded with her teasingly biting his penis head. Lorna swung herself over his arched chest. Facing him, she bent backwards, supported by her elbows, which lay either side of his body, and pushed her vagina outward and towards his mouth.

part one

"Taste the sweetness and feel the delight!" She purred, stoned.

He extended his tongue, not forcefully, but gently. Allowing it to run around the outside. Using just the tip, he slid his tongue onto the clitoris, flicking it once or twice lightly, invoking her moans and inviting her to want more. The pleasure of sex was with them all. Lorna's raised, arched body felt the right hand of Jen slide its way up along her leg, across and around her thigh and between her buttocks. Jen's fingers felt his tongue, flicking with rhythm upon Lorna's clitoris but retreated away from this moist area, in search of her anus.

"Play with me!" Lorna gasped, as Jen's fingers worked their way into her anal-hole.

With Lorna being serviced by oral and hand simulation it did not take her too long for her reach her orgasm. As she quickened her rhythmic pace the other two lovers flowed with the motion. Jen's fingers were pushing up to the knuckle, moving in a harmony with Lorna's own body. He, on the other hand, wouldn't comply fully with her request and sought to deny her the right to reach such a pleasurable height sexually.

"You bastard!" She yelled, "wait until its your fucking turn" and with this she forced her own left hand down between her legs and, ignoring his still working tongue, pushed two fingers upon her own clitoris and began to rub, slowly at first but working them quickly up to full speed. As she reached her orgasm she pushed her vagina further forward and began to rub it up against his face. Jen's rhythm was constant and unrelenting as her fingers slid effortlessly in and out of Lorna's anus.

"Too slow!" Lorna said, realising and relieved. "Lick away!" Her own fingers were removed and she pressed herself harder down upon his face, using his nose to finalise the orgasm. Jen removed her fingers, as the pace slowed. Lorna rolled to one side and ran her hand from his chest, down to his pubic hair and then back up again, resting it upon his chest. Her thumb and fore-finger rubbed themselves against his right nipple, sometimes, intentionally, trapping his hardened tips between the two fingers.

Below, squatted between his 'V' shaped legs Jen was bobbling up and down on his penis still. He had already realised that Lorna's other, free hand, was working its way between Jen's legs but had reached far beyond the point of caring for anyone but himself. He closed his eyes, imagined the vastness and the insignificance of ourselves and the universe. In fact, none of this stopped him from ejaculating his semen over Jen's face and in her mouth. The two girls kissed one another, licking at the lip smeared semen as they exchanged bodily fluids. He began to masturbate, erecting his penis once again.

part one

The two girls rolled onto the mattress, indulging and enjoying each gentle touch administered. He wasn't jealous, it turned him on in fact, but he did feel left out. Rolling onto his side, facing the two girls, he began to stroke their bodies.

"Feeling left out?" Lorna questioned.

"Umh! Just a little. You don't mind do you?" The question was rhetorical more than anything else. After all this session was made for three.

"Ah! Oh God! Yes!" Lorna replied. "You know what I want, just give it to me!"

Positions changed. Jen lay back upon the bed, her hands clasping at the headboard behind her. Lorna placed herself between Jen's legs, her head lowered. She ran her tongue around her naval a few times before allowing her tongue to enter Jen's pubic region and eventually her vagina.

"Maybe," Lorna mumbled, "we should strap her to the bed and both rape her?" She looked up at him as he began to position himself behind her.

"Later, perhaps," was the only reply as, kneeling upon the bed, he held onto Lorna's hips and began to insert his penis into her pussy. She groaned at each entry and exit.

Positions are changed again. Jen brought her knees up, with the help of Lorna, to a position where her anus was easily reached by Lorna's already searching tongue. Her position over emphasised her anus, but then she knew that already. He, sensing her change of need, withdrew his penis from Lorna and inserted into her anus as far as it would enter.

"Umh! Now that's what I wanted," she giggled as it slid in and out.

Three people satisfying not only themselves but each other also. The sex seemed to flow and twist forever. Ejaculation after ejaculation followed as newer, more unusual, positions were dreamt up. It couldn't get any better than this, he thought. He wanted it to continue to flow forever but knew that it wouldn't and so drank up all that he could. His thoughts were along way from the mirrors and reflected images of self that he so often sought sexual gratification in. However, even within this scenario, if he had looked deeper or beyond the event, examined his truth, but then again, as so often, he would have recognised a familiar loneliness that would resist and not go away. A loneliness that never grew and yet, never reached into his life fully either. It merely lurked amongst the backdrops.

MASTER OF GAMES - II

"I think we need some more wine in here!" Peter shouted through to the kitchen. "Claire? Can you hear me?" He pushed his seated body further across the table, towards the kitchen door. "Claire! Hello!"

Andrew slid his chair back from the table, raising a hand as he did so. "Forget it. I'm on it," he said as he swung away and up from the table. "Red or white?"

"White," Peter replied, reclining back once again and re-focusing upon the joint that lay before him. Andrew looked around the table but no one else seemed to have any specific preference to wine and so he passed into the galley kitchen.

Claire was there. Dancing to herself as she stirred the sauce for the pasta, a cigarette in her non-stirring hand. Andrew drew passed her, towards the kitchen's end where the refrigerator lived, commenting as he did so.

"Smells god. How long to dinner?"

"Five minutes," she dazily replied as Andrew opened the fridge door, squatting downward in search.

"So, How's it going?"

"Fine. Five more minutes."

"No, no, not the pasta, you. You and Mike." Andrew took a bottle from the fridge and rose as he did so. Claire didn't face him, remaining concentrated upon her stirring, her dancing stopped.

"Not so good actually," She drew upon her cigarette. "I don't reckon on it continuing much longer. Mike is, er, I don't know, kinda distant. You know?" Andrew began to uncork the wine. "Sometimes I think he'd rather be with someone else. He just..", she shrugged, "just doesn't seem to like me."

"What about you?" Andrew said turning his head towards her. "What do you want?"

For the first time Claire looked away from the sauce mixture, stubbing out her cigarette, she faced him. "I want somebody to talk to," she said.

The moment, for that was clearly what it was, one of *those* moments, shattered as the cork popped clear of the bottle. It didn't shatter the conversation however, just the eye contact.

"Claire, if you want to talk, just ask me. You know I'm there for you. Anytime, just give me a call, you know that. If I can help I will." He clasped the wine bottle.

part one

Claire had long since returned to her constant stirring of the sauce.

"Anytime?"

"Anytime."

"Thanks," she just said as Andrew once again drew himself passed her. He dropped his free hand upon her right shoulder.

"No problem, just ask," he concluded re-entering into the dining room.

It was Carey's dining room, it was Carey's house. But then it always was. Never anyone else's house, just Carey's. Three or four evenings a week, 7 p.m. until the last one dropped. Always Carey's. Carey was Claire's mother, a 60s throw back. Art school educated, the epitome of the drug culture. Blonde, beautiful and oozing life through skin that under-estimated her age. Her house typified her persona. Stylish yet both intriguing and fun also. Andrew and Donna, Mike and Claire, Peter and his girlfriend, Lara and the mother of the household, Carey. Dinner was causal, everyone knew the boundaries of the others and they rarely crossed. No one, however, could fail to observe the sometimes tension laden words exchanged by Mike and Claire that cut, rather than flowed, through the dinner conversation.

Dinner was followed by cards. Gin Rummy in fact. The two lowest scores did the washing up. The game was slow, drearily so, points hard to score and the only event was the eventual outcome. Mike and Peter lost and got to spend the next hour in the kitchen. The others, wine and hashish filled, reclined around the table, or made their way towards the fire in the next room. Andrew and Claire entered the fire room, collapsed upon the sofa which was up against the back wall, promptly followed by Carey, who sat upon a stool next to the fire, her back towards them. Donna and Lara remained, engaged deeply. Carey flicked some ash into the flames before looking away from the fire, at Claire and Andrew.

She extended her arm. "Joint?"

"No! No! No more!" Claire exclaimed. "My head is spinning already."

"Cheers," Andrew said as he partly climbed off the sofa to collect the gift. Carey, having passed her offering, returned to the comfort of the dancing flames and the sanctity of inner thought. Andrew took two puffs. As he did so he drew his legs up onto the sofa and adjusted his body posture in a manner that made him face Claire.

"You sure you don't want some?" Andrew said to Claire, casting an eye towards the joint.

part one

"Ah, no thanks" Long pause. She lifted her head towards him. "Can we talk now?"

"Yeah sure. Now is good. I'm a little trashed but, yeah, sure. What's up?"

"I'm just thinking that's all. What if I were to say that I no longer loved Mike and that I wished that he would move out of this house?"

Andrew looked briefly towards Carey but her nights in take had rendered her incapable of conversation and, seemingly, of eaves dropping.

"Why do you say this?" Andrew asked trying to pass the joint once again.

"Its just the way I'm feeling at the moment. He annoys me. I'm actually looking forward to him going off to this bike course for the week, just to get some peace and space."

"You'll miss him though I bet, when he's gone I mean. He's kinda like a puppy that no one wants but is loveable all the same. Why don't you just see how the weeks break goes? Maybe it will change your feelings."

Claire took the joint this time when it as offered. "Yeah, I know you're right but I don't think that anything will change by his not being here."

"Okay, let's take stock shall we? What are you going to do without him? I mean, you guys have been together for so long that 'Mike and Claire' is one singular word. Its, what's the word I'm looking for, a given. Its a natural combination."

"Well, things change. I'm not even sure how he feels. He talks to you. Maybe you could shed some light upon this?" She dragged her fingers through her hair. "He must talk to you?"

"Claire, hold on here! I'm not going to deny that Mike and I talk but I don't want to get caught in this. I talk to Mike and I talk to you. Both I treat with trust and respect. Ask me questions if you want but I may not be able to answer them fully." He reclaimed the joint and inhaled deeply. "I don't want to take sides but I will, at least, try to be honest to those question raised."

"I just want to know how he feels! That's all."

"Strangely enough he asked the same thing yesterday, in the pub. It seems to me that you are both on rocky ground here. I know that Mike is hard to talk to but you have to try if you're to get any answers to your questions."

"Just tell me what he said!"

part one

"Look, fine, if you want me to talk straight then I will. I my opinion, and I stress 'my', you and Mike need to separate for a while. To find yourselves as singular entities. You know? People in your own right. I reckon, for what it is worth that both you and Mike have forgotten who you are as individuals. Here's a question that I think you should consider. What do you hope for in the next couple of years? Project yourself based upon now and see if its really what you want." He snuggled further into the sofa, casting an arm upon the back. His other hand flicked the ash in the general direction of the ash tray. "Does that make sense?"

"Yeah. I'd never thought about it in that way before. Just as a day to day thing. I think that at the moment I don't see Mike within my images."

"Think about it for a while at least. "

"I'm not really sure that I need to think about it. I have a gut feeling, you know? I know deep inside that it is over. It just seems to be, you know, I'm use to having him around."

"There will be others," Andrew replied, placing the joint into the ash tray. "Find yourself first before answering such questions. Separate the unit down to singular wants and desires."

"Right. Yeah, I'll try but its not an easy thing to ask."

"Claire, this is my opinion of it all that's all. If I was in your shoes that's what I'd be doing but you are you and as such must make your own roadway to walk upon."

"Sometimes," she said out of the blue, "I image kissing, having sex, with other people. People I think care. My roadway has to be dual carriage. I need someone there with me."

"Sure, that's fine but look only at your lane. Boyfriends, girlfriends, these things come and go. Find your 'true' direction no matter how it affects you. I mean, what do you want?"

"My house, this house, Carey, my business as a success, that sort of stuff."

"So why do you need a man in the equation?"

"Its just what I want. What I've always needed."

"Perhaps its time to change this feeling. Clearly you need to if you want to get anywhere. Achieve your goals. Short of marriage to some one rich and into horses, it would seem, you know, that these are things you must do alone without support. Its dragging you down not up. You're not in control of this relationship Mike is. Regain it and you may find that being single will allow you be all that you want to be.. Look, all I'm saying is use this break wisely."

part one

"Can I still talk to you about..." Mike and Peter entered the room. Both carried a joint and a bottle of wine.

"Who's up for more?" Peter questioned enthusiastically. He was normally the last to fall. It stopped the conversation dead between Andrew and Claire and the flow of other conversations began to take shape. Donna and Lara entered the room a little later. Carey, the only real worker, retired to bed leaving just the six to discuss things that outside of the drug and alcohol context made no real sense and, yet, it filled three hours of their lives.

Claire did not say much. The tension was still there between her and Mike but the drugs had made it more healable for both themselves and the others. Andrew, game on and in full swing, made infrequent eye contact with Claire, which she returned with a smile and then would glance away. At this point Andrew knew that he could have Claire given a few more sessions. The game was clearly in full production and time and timing would ensure a 'safe' play, as he called it.

The rest of the evening continued without a hitch, Peter and Andrew were the only functioning people, even if worse for wear, and the conversation was easy. There was only one point that is worthy of note; the issue with Claire that was raised by Peter.

"Claire and Mike seemed hassled," he enquired.

"Aren't all relationships that way?" Andrew laughed.

"Not like this. I feel sorry for them both. I love them both equally."

"What's the score with you and Claire? Andrew bluntly asked.

"In what way?"

"In the way that it seems you are chasing her."

"Fuck off! She wants me I reckon and, to be honest, I'm flattered and tempted were it not for Mike and Lara."

"So, you're not interested by her playing?" Andrew asked, looking for a more direct answer.

"I like her and that, but she's not for me. I'd fuck her given the chance but nothing else."

"You'd cheat on Lara?"

"If the mood took me. I'd feel guilty, a little, by it but nothing else. Its no big deal."

"I beg to differ. Even know I understand the point. Its just that Claire seems such easy prey at the moment and, well, you seem to be enjoying the chase."

part one

"So what? Its not going to lead anywhere. I like the thrill." Andrew yawned as Peter spoke.

"God, I'm pissed, " Andrew exclaimed, "I'm off to bed, if you don't mind?"

"Night."

"Good night and happy drinking," Andrew said as he left the room with a smile. Possibly, it was a drunken smile but, however, it was more likely a smile of knowing. Playing games was, he was without doubt, the best thing in his life and boy was he good.

THE BOOK OF HURT – Pt3

October 1999

***Sunday* 17**

    I am writing this diary entry as an evening log. They had wanted to see me. My door portal opened and closed with a depressing frequency. By this morning, and through a lack of sleeping, I had become progressively paranoid by the constant flapping of the screen. It did cease, eventually, just after 7 o'clock but by that time the damage had been done. What do these people want from me? I still haven't truly been out of my room and maybe that was their concern. Eventually, around 10.30 am there had been a knock at my door, a quick peek, and then the door opened.

"You okay?"

"Yeah, yeah. Just enjoying my own company."

"You sure you don't want to leave your room?"

"Yes."

"Anyhow, its your choice. The doctor will see you in about a hour. Okay?"

"Sure." It wasn't okay of course. This morning, as now, I don't need doctors probing my mind, dishing out drugs like sweets and examining me. Now that I have actually experienced it, this diary entry is an evening log, I remain even more convinced. As I'd walked into his office I'd become aware that this meeting would not be a mutual joining of minds. Instead, I had just sat completely dumbfounded and dazed by his very presence.

It went something like this.

"Please sit down."

"Thanks."

"So, how is it going? What's been happening?"

"Er, well, I'm sure you are aware of why I'm here. Its going pretty shit really. I thought about taking an overdose just before coming here and since then things have been, what's the word? Umh! slipping."

"You seem confused?"

"I've no idea at all about how I, er, got here really. I just rather lost my way a little and..."

"And this was after the operation?" He enquired, looking at his notes.

"Yeah, but, this had been building for sometime before that. Decades, I'd say."

He sat forward, I sat back. "Although strange that it happened after the operation isn't it?" It was more a reference rather than a questioning sentence.

He continued. "So, you did the test yesterday? (Damn. I forgot to comment on the psycho-analytical test) .You've talked to the ward doctor and I have a fair idea about how you feel."

"You do?" I had only seen the ward doctor for a matter of minutes and even then it was family background stuff.

"Yes. Yes. I believe that you need to terms with the operation. You need to look at the issues that this surgery has brought up. It clearly is at the root of your problem. I'm not really set-up for the type of therapy that you require. I know somewhere that can..."

"But, er, I don't what to get involved with pyscho-theraphy. All they do is drag up your past. I'm only here for a rest, my doctor told me so. "

"No, no, no! As far as I am aware you are here to be treated. I'll prescribe some pills to help you cope and refer you to this other place."

part one

I argued about it for a further ten minutes before concluding that this was going nowhere. I desired to conclude this conversation before I really said something that I'd regret.

"Okay," he said, "if you don't go to this place, well, lets just weigh up these options. If you now attempt to leave this hospital we will section you. If you refuse to go to another hospital for treatment we may section you. I've also spoken to your surgical consultant and he's in complete agreement." He sat back in his chair, twiddling a pencil in both hands which occasionally involved him putting it under his nose, as if imitating a moustache.

"So, you've really got me nailed, haven't you? Fucked if I do and fucked if I don't." I was so angry at this point. I think it was partly because I was no longer in control or, upon reflection, because they clearly were not listening to me. "I didn't come here so you could fuck my life up." I started to cry. "I came to get some help for fucks sake." The anger grew.

"This is shit," I continued. "You've known me ten minutes and you give me medication and pack me off to some other fucking place. I have no wish to go." I gripped the chair's arms, as if attempting to leave. "You don't have a fucking clue, do you?" Idiot. "Typical textbook thoughts. No concern for the individual. Treat them all the same!

Pump them up with drugs so that they'll not misbehave and send them back out. And for what?"

I stood up. "This is over. You've really fucked me up now. Everything is tainted by your fucking interference. Bollocks to this." And I was gone.

Now, here I am. Writing this shit down because it happened. I'm stuck in this psychiatric ward and, seemingly, they can do what they want. My doctor lied to me. Made me feel secure and then dumped me into a pit of hell. Not only is this place hell but so are the people in it. Well, those that I've seen anyhow. I am scared to death of this place. I've tried to rationalise this but I can no longer put up with it. I've spent all day long dealing with the issues raised by the consultant and I still feel nailed to the wall. I don't want any of the choices. But I also don't want to be sectioned just for this, that really would fuck me up.

All this said, my options can be seen as limited; specialist, here or section if I leave. I quite like the idea of 'none of the above'. It has an air of defiance. It suggests that I can do whatever I want to without outsider pressure. I am also scared because 'none of the above' means taking my life and ending it all. Not that its a problem for me. I find a appeal about it. What life can I have at the moment? Future projections are bleak, the present merely depresses me and my past has been hell.

options.
> ~~a) Specialist hospital.~~
> ~~b) here and section~~
> c) suicide

Seemingly, option 'c' is the best. Outside in the corridor a fight is breaking out. All this merely serves to increase my need for option 'c'. I don't belong here. I'm not like them because I am not mad. I maybe here but I'm not mad in the same way. Okay, plump for option 'c'. I'm not sure how I'm going to do this though. I've always thought about taking pills but getting hold of them would take forever. So, that's out. Hanging is the other way that doesn't seem that bad. I don't know how I'll achieve this either though as there is nothing to hang from in this damn room. I need a plan and I need it pretty quick before I get carted off. It seems strange to select suicide over either staying here or going some place else but that really only serves to demonstrate just how fucked up I really am.

FLESH OF DREAMS (3)

This time she came via a knock upon the door. same door, same room, same hotel, same dream. She had a sphere with her, held within her left hand. It looked like the one I held, only it had different colours. Her's was more 'earthy', as if supporting life. Through the globe were colours of green, brown and blue. White circled around the sphere's circumference in spirals. Mine, on the other hand, contained colours of purple and red and looked thick and heavy internally. She made no effort to re-introduce herself, merely walked into the room once the door was fully open.

"So, you're back?" She nodded towards the globe. "Have you seen yourself within the globe?" I went to answer but she continued regardless. "No. I can see quite clearly that you have not seen. Do you even know yet what it is?"

"A planet?" I guessed, expecting her mocking tone to follow.

"Umh! Well, yes in a way it is. This," she extended her arm to highlight the sphere, "is mine and what you hold is yours. Quite different and, yet, the same." She walked towards the centre of the room. "I think the time has come to explain all. If you think you're ready that is?"

part one

I looked at the object held within my hands, Quite pretty yet it also contained a cautionary air. It wasn't beautiful, like hers, and I wondered why this was.

"How can I tell when I'm ready when I don't know what it is you wish to share with me?" I sat down upon the sofa. She sat on one opposite, separated by a coffee table.

Okay," She said, "I guess its time for the lessons to begin." She bent forward and placed her globe upon the coffee table. "We, that is all of us within the Shore Hotel, hold the sphere. It is a part of us. It is changed by us and it, in turn, changes us. There is a bond via the emotions that we hold. Yet, the globe is about progression. It changes through time and contact. Yours is a planet just developing, whilst mine has been supporting life essences for a millennia. Your globe, if nurtured, will develop as mine has done. Okay? So far?

"Ah, no. Why do we carry these things?"

"You still don't know who you are do you? You have no idea where you lie. What is before you and why you are here. Do you?"

"I believe I know why I am here. I'm here because I am on a mission to discover myself. Who exactly it is I am and where I am at." I must confess the hotel, this woman, made no sense in terms of my quest. "I don't understand the hotel, you, the globe but I know that it has something to do with what I seek. You're here to help me achieve my sense of what and who I am. Aren't you?"

"Okay," she picked up her planet and spun it in her hands, "back to basics. The hotel is a resting place. You called yourself here. You needed to escape the blackness and the space that you find yourself living in. You called yourself here because you needed a place to rest and think. The Shore Hotel gives you this. It is a dream state. No, it is more than that, it is a bridge between that which is real and that of dreams. It is a hotel because, well, because the is how you choose to see and experience it. Others, no all, see their own "Shore". It is their memories that create it."

"And do they all carry globes?" I asked.

"Oh yes. They all carry globes in various states of development."

"So, okay, let me grab a hold upon this," I said excitedly. "This is a place where I can find out who, what I am?"

"Exactly. Now to move on, if I may?" I gestured yes with a nod. "Everybody within the Shore is here for the same reason. That is, to find themselves."

"And the globes?"

"The planets, call them what you will," she shrugged, "are to be nurtured. When it brings forth life your questions will be visible within it. You will be able to focus upon yourself within it, to see where, what and who you are. It will lead you out of your darkness and into the real world where you belong."

"Right. I understand so far, but how long does this take?"

"That depends on what you wish to see and on how fast you create it. There is no time as you expect it."

"So, what you are saying, and correct me if I am wrong, is that I am here, in this hotel, to generate a planet that is exactly like my real world and, that once this is completed I will be able to focus within the globe and find out exactly where, who, what I am and the this will free me from the blackness into the real world," I gulped for breath, "is this right?"

"Great, so far."

"You mean there's more?"

Oh yes. Just a little, so bear with it." She made herself more comfortable upon the sofa, reclining back and stretching both arms across and out from it. "Here's the best part."

I moved my position for the first time. Sitting forward, arms upon knees, globe still firmly gripped. "Continue, please," I said.

"Right. There are within this hotel many like me. Call us teachers if you like. Some, like myself, will guide you through this confusing time and, hopefully, release you. However, you may encounter other teachers who will try and entice you. Offer you quicker ways to achieve your aim. Offer you something special or exciting. Do not trust these."

There was a forcefulness within her voice.. "Do not trust them for they are not true teachers. They, like myself, are there because you want them to be but they come from the darker side of you. Not from the true you, the you that wants to be released. Ignore these teachers for they will destroy your planet and you only get one chance. They will make you look into your globe before it is ready for inspection. Such actions are bad, really bad."

"But why?" I ask naively.

"Because, how can I put this, because you will not see the real you, as and where you are now. You may end up seeing a past you or, even worse, a self that exists only within an ancestor. As I said, you only get one chance to become real again. Looking too soon will leave you here forever. Trust no other but me. Avoid anyone else. Are you willing to do this?"

"Of course I am." I was a little insulted. "I'm here to escape this blackness that surrounds me."

"Good. Now, where's your planet?"

I uncupped my hands in front of my face. I am still sitting forwards, arms upon my knees, with a face that holds on to a promise.

"Cup you hands around the globe again and remember do not look too deeply, not yet. Cup your hands please."

I obey the instruction.

"Now close your eyes and free your mind."

Slap! She hits me hard.

I awaken to a similar state of affairs. I try, this time, not to think about the dream I have just had in order to eradicate the sense of urgency that I feel. The droning is back, no better or worse than it was before . It just goes on and on like some form of Japanese water torture. Slowly, I'm convinced, I am being driven to the point of insanity by its constant barrage. I am still seeking that name but it doesn't seem to crop up anymore. I can only conclude that it is lost forever. Yet, I keep on longing. I need this name, need it badly. I need to find its meaning. Its my only contact with the outside, beyond me is blackness and, wait, listen. I hear something else. Another name, something that I recognise not so much to do with myself but within my vocabulary. It is definitely a pro-noun but it casts no images like the other name. Yet, anyhow, I recognise it quite clearly.

I heard the word "Andrew" and that as all.

FLIGHT OF FANTASY

flight, flight - into fantasy
wings that glide - over wintered mountain
carpeted pure white - containing memories
thoughts caught - within flakes of time
snow covered dreams - songs of heartache
rested and frozen - lying still
gliding through openness - one eye constant
I'm easy prey - preying for the easy
picking up dreams - but leaving their traces
for others to recreate
in the fullness of time
flight, flight - into fantasy
everything we touch is placed this way
easy - forgetful - unimportant
experience - hidden - but not disappeared
and as I swoop down to my prey
there lying
I catch familiar thoughts- frozen in time
and thaw them out in the back of my mind

part two

"passion displays
with ice and desire"

FROM WITHOUT TO WITHIN

standing upon the outside
I am a reflection looking in
listening to others
talking in tongues
words that I once held
cupped within memories
that have long since decayed
leaving me monosyllabic
leaving me disjointed
and unable to express
my words of wisdom
which have changed with age
and a mental failure
fallen and trashed
into demented verse
and I am lonely here
amongst these people
my presence just felt
like ripples in a pond
I cast my self outwards
but still no one listens
to the ramblings I speak
talk of hurt and pain
fail to become noticed
and I retract to react
to the uneasiness of my position
placing myself further from that which is central
I circle with a fear
that none can ever know
for no one is listening to the rhythms upon the margins
desperately hollow - standing upon the outside
I am a reflection looking in
pressed to the screen

part two

I hear no words - I am a stranger
I am strange and devoid
importance emphasised by my position
I know there is nobody here
within this place
where I fail even to recognise myself
shallow and open
I am the reflection of what I have been

TO HELL WITH UNCERAINTY [c]

"**Y**ou dirty little fucker," he whispered. "This is too much even for you."

He was lying upon a bed. Not his bed but a friend's bed. On loan for the weekend in the country. He'd taken with him a girl he had picked up at a local night-spot. She probably wouldn't be everyone's choice but she was his. Slightly overweight, she oozed charisma through the rolls of fat. He liked her, when they had first me. She always contained a smile that suggested a true happiness. He'd been seeing her for a week before this trip away. Wanting to take her somewhere special , so that her loss of virginity would always be a memory. A pleasant memory for her to carry forever. For him, well, it was purely a new experience.

It was getting dark outside, which seemed to heighten both of their sexual selves. They'd cooked a meal, which had been eaten and drunk beside the open fire. The effects couldn't have been more cliché but it seemed to work.

"This is nice," she said, "just the two of us and the fire and all that."

"Yeah, nice." He was blunt. Uninterested and contained by a over whelming urge to have sex. He got up and knelt beside her, stroking the side of her face with his hand.

She looked up as he did so and smiled. He bent further down and kissed her upon the lips.

"Do we need coffee?" He enquired.

"No. Not coffee, just you."

"I am yours to do with what you will," he said and smiled.

They didn't bother with the bed at first. Kissing each other, they stripped naked in front of the fire. Another cliché but a truth none the less. Kneeling and facing each other they continued to kiss. Deep, longing kisses that held desperation and anticipation simultaneously. His tongue entered her mouth, hers stroking his. Hands ran back and forth, both of them avoiding contact with genitalia. Cupping breasts, stroking skin and occasionally licking each other around that face and neck area. As they stroked and licked his mouth began to make its way to the breast area. His tongue licked at her left nipple. Flicking it gently forcing it to become hard and causing him to turn his attention to the other breast. He drew his left hand up to her left breast, catching a nipple between his finger and thumb, squeezing slightly. Soon both nipples had become firm. He drew away, back up to her face and her awaiting mouth. Her hands ran across his chest.

He knew that he would have to make the first move. She would never do it. Her experience was seriously limited.

So he did so. Dropping free the hand that had been stroking at her breast, he ran it down towards her pubic hair. He could sense, without even touching her vagina, the she was very wet and welcoming. He could sense it both within her moist public hair and within the noises that she made as he stroked her. Her hand followed his. Moving away from his chest and sliding downwards. He was quite surprised to it run over the head of his erection and down onto his testicles. She'd moved faster than him. Entering a region of his body that he'd thought she would fear to go. He smiled. She was obviously game and ready for what was , unspoken, going to happen. This time he followed her and slid two fingers down between her legs and began to stroke her clitoris.

"I want you now," she demand.

"Not yet, its too soon."

"Now!" She repeated.

Andrew slid his middle finger towards her awaiting virginal opening, feeling as he did so her spare hand dropping on to his.

"No. Not that way."

"Why? What's wrong?"

part two

"Nothing. Well, you'll find it strange."

"Try me," he said.

"Its just that, well, just that I want, oh God, I'm so embrassed."

"Go on," he urged.

"Its just that," sharp in-take of breath, "Its just that I want your penis to be the first thing to enter me, that's all." She giggled with embarrassment.

He withdrew his hand and, using both hands, cupped her face. He kissed her upon the lips.

"That's okay. Its fine. I aim to please, especially you. Its not a problem and certainly nothing to be embrassed about." He laughed. "We can play later, we have all night."

"Sorry."

"Shush, not another word."

She lay upon her back, legs open, awaiting the moment she would remember forever. He positioned himself, kneeling between her legs. He didn't lie on top of her as he wanted to see his penis penetrate her virginal hole. Slowly he edged it into her. He wasn't quite sure what he expected, a tight entrance, a need to break through, he wasn't sure. In fact, it was none of these things. Although slightly tight to enter there were no real problems encountered. He positioned himself on top of her, disappointed at the lack of experience felt, and began to go through the motions. It wasn't great sex. No. It wasn't even poor. Penetration to him was cheap and easy to come by. There was no experience with it. It was just actions. Actions that he found vulgar and dis-interesting. It didn't take her long to reach orgasm anyhow. Four or five minutes and it was over. Andrew faked his, just to put an end to this charade called sex. He lifted himself off her and she reached for a cigarette, which she lit upon the fire. Seemingly, it was over for a while, at least for her. He watched he smoking, inhaling and exhaling, and began to wonder why people make such a fuss over virgin sex.

She finished her cigarette whilst looking at him.

"Is it all over?" she questioned.

"Only if you want it to be."

"No way! I've waited 17 years for this."

"Okay, so its not over." Came the reply.

"Goody. Can I suck you?"

part two

"You need to ask?"

"I thought I ought to."

"Don't ask, just do it. Its better that way."

"Okay."

She sucked him as he lay upon his back. The head of his penis in her mouth, her two hands around the length. She was good, must better than he has expected and within minutes he was squirting his semen into the back of her mouth.

"Climb on," he said.

So she did. Straddled across him, he felt more turned on. Her breasts bounced before him as his hands slid around her body. She moaned a pleasurable tone that signalled an approval to continue. He was glad at this moan. It could have gone one of two ways. Either she would be viled by his sexual requirements or accept them. She, he decided, would be the former.

After several minutes of this he noticed her slow down her rhythm. He had his eyes closed before this moment but right now they were open.

"What's wrong?" The tone held concern.

"I'm bleeding."

He looked down at their entwined genitals. The length of his penis, that was visible, was stained red. Even his pubic hair. She had blood upon her thighs.

"What's wrong?" she quizzed.

"Nothing. Its fine. It happens sometimes the first time around. Don't worry."

"Are you sure?" Doubt cast.

"Do you trust me?" He asked.

"Yes."

"Then relax."

They changed positions. He found a new excitement within the introduction of blood. A fresh drive within himself to taste her truly. She was now lying upon the floor, legs spread, whilst he knelt between her thighs and began to lick at her clitoris. As he did so he played with himself. He had never tasted anybody else's blood before and it turned him on. He worked his tongue inside her, his face pressed within her thighs, happily licking at the juices flowing from within her. He could taste the blood. Desired it even. Bringing his hands up towards her face,

part two

he parted her thighs further. His hands, purposefully, ran over her thighs and stomach. Smearing the blood across her flesh. The licking ceased. He now knelt before her and, taking his penis into his right hand, began to rub it against her, coating it in a layer of red.

"You still want to suck me?"

"Ummh!" her eyes were closed.

He then straddled her. Holding onto his penis he began to rub it along her lips, outlining the mouth. The blood resembled lipstick, deep and glossy. He outlined one last time before inserting it into her awaiting mouth. As she sucked, he placed a hand behind himself and began to rub her clitoris. He continued to smear the blood, bringing his hand forward and working across breasts, dying then red.

"I want to lick you clean. I want to smear this entire room and lick it clean." He removed his penis from her mouth. "I also want to fuck your arse. Would you like that?"

"Ummh! Do you need to ask?" She mimicked.

So he did. Working his was around her he began to lick the blood off her body, masturbating whilst doing so. Occasionally he would tease her by rubbing her clitoris briefly or by inserting his fingers into her arse. It was certainly clear that she was enjoying it as she arched and swayed to her rhythms, indulging in climax after climax.

"Get upon your hands and knees." It was a demand more than anything else but she happily did so. He took his penis and began to insert it into her anus. She gave a moan as he fucked her arse and the more he did the more she moaned.

He didn't climax inside her. He withdrew before and slid his semen filled cock into her mouth. She took it without protest.

This time it was he who stopped. He fell to one side and began to roll a joint.

"Jesus! That was good."

"So, that's sex is it?"

"Ummh! You didn't enjoy it?" he asked.

"Oh, I loved it. All of it. I don't regret this nor will I ever. Fancy going again?"

"After this," he said, raising the joint.

"I can wait," came the reply.

"Good."

In the light of morning he awoke first. He looked at her lying in the bed. A bed steeped in semen, blood and urine. It had been one hell of a night and, he had to admit, the best he had ever had possibly. He lay back down again.

"You dirty little fucker," he whispered. "This really is too much even for you."

THE MASTER OF GAMES – III

A quietness followed the evening of the meal between Andrew and Claire. Any communication had a sharp edge to it, as if somewhere, something, had been said that ought not to. For Andrew it had been expected. Claire's confession' about her feelings for Mike were bound to cause a temporary state of confusion. For Claire it was the prospect of other people finding out through the gossip vines. As far as Andrew was concerned the knowing was the true starting of the game. Her feelings were known to him, her weakness made her susceptible to manipulation and, yet, it also required subtle, careful approach. Even smiles exchanged between the two were careful and nervous. Yet, there remained within all this confession and embarrassment there remained something glittering within their exchanges. Something that suggested and acknowledged a sense of togetherness. Moments shared. Such awkwardness would diminish, Andrew was sure of the, and when it did the moves would be played out.

Days past where no boundaries were broken. Tentative, frustrated days that hinted at distrust and denial even though Andrew had told no one of their conversation. Why would he have done so? Such information was useful, ammunition, and, most importantly, it was something shared. Claire had trusted him and, for this particular game to work, it was important to retain this trust. Time was everything.

He was right no to push or challenge her. Within a week the looks and exchanges had become as they were before. Their relationship returned, perhaps it was stronger as a consequence but that didn't really matter. What mattered was the reopening of their communication. It was part of the game and Andrew knew that it would happen eventually. If prompted he could even have predicted the nature of the conversation. The 'where' didn't matter but, to help paint the scene, it had been in a public house where the usual group, minus Donna and Lara, often met. Peter and Mike were in the back room playing pool which left just Claire and Andrew. A position that made conversation inevitable anyhow. The ice-breaker was provided by Andrew.

"I seem to be sensing, er, something. No. The feeling that you wished you hadn't talked to me."

"You seem sad about it," she replied.

"Well, it has upset me. It seems as if you don't trust me to keep our conversations secret. I haven't told anyone, if that is what you think. I thought you trusted me?"

I do. I, er, just, look all I can say is sorry. I'm confused by what's going on. I feel as if someone has turned me inside out. You know?"

"Listen Claire. We can talk if you want to but if you don't then, well, its no big deal. You're a friend, a close friend, and I'm here to help if you need it."

"Thanks," she took a drink, "I'm hoping that Mike going away on this bike course tomorrow will ease my feelings. What do you think?"

Andrew placed an arm around her shoulders and squeezed her reassuringly. "What do I think? As I said the other day you should use this time. Not just as a space to feel relaxed in but also to see you future prospects more clearly, without, you know, outside interests."

"Well, nothing has changed since we last spoke." She put down her glass. "Can I ask for something, well, stupid?"

"Umh, you can ask but I can't promise anything."

"I, erm, I just feel that, " tears swelled in her eyes. Andrew's face changed from caring listener to concerned friend.

"What is it?"

"Oh, fuck it! I just feel that I need a hug, that's all. Stupid really. Isn't it?"

part two

Andrew drew his other arm round her and pulled her closer to him. "I don't think that its stupid. We all need hugs at some point."

She rested her head upon his shoulder, sliding her arms around his waist as she do so. Andrew buried his face into her hair and smelt her loveliness. "I'll always be here for you."

She began to cry into his shoulder. "Hey! Hey! What's all this about? Are you feeling that bad?"

"I'm on the edge. I can't cope anymore. I just want to see some happiness in my life. Mike and I just don't share our, er, moments like we use to. Have you ever been in love and felt lonely at the same time?"

Andrew relaxed the embrace. "I believe the term is disillusionment. You're just hanging onto a past that has died. Your 'love' seems to me to be merely an attachment rather than any real love."

"I know," Claire shrugged. "I'm sorry I treated you so badly. You've helped me a lot. Helped me clear some cob-webs and think at a level I hadn't considered." There was a pause. Still and calm. She drew her head from his shoulder. "I love you," she said. Andrew's heart pumped faster at the mention of these three words. "I love you because some how you are there for me, always."

"That's just the way I am. I care for you a great deal. I hate to see you like this." He kissed the top of her head. "I just want to care for you."

They broke the embrace and both reached for their drinks.

"So, Mike goes tomorrow?"

"Yep," she shrugged.

"And who's going to fill the void? It seems you need someone."

"I thought that was your job!" She took a cigarette from its packet and lit it. Blowing out the smoke she said, "I'd like you to fill the void if, er, you don't mind that is?"

"What a surrogate boyfriend?"

"Just a friend that cares would be nice. I'm not inviting you to bed or anything."

"I should hope not!" Andrew laughed. "I'm a married man practically."

"So, you and Donna are doing well?"

"I never said that. Its going but I'm just not sure where."

part two

"Will you stay the week at my house whilst Mike is away?"

""On the sofa you mean?"

"Yeah, of course on the sofa. Although I'm sure we can find you somewhere more comfortable."

"Okay, yeah, why not! I could do with a breakaway from my house. Are you going to play the maid or what? I'll only stay if you treat me like a king." He laughed again.

"I'm not sure about that but I'll cook you breakfast. That's my limit."

"Yeah, sure. Why not. Sounds better that anything else I've been offered."

"Think Donna will be okay with it?"

"Yeah, sure. She's on some training thing at the moment anyhow. You know, a nurse thing, so I doubt she'd even notice. "Okay honey, then let's do it." Claire sounded excited at the prospect. Andrew retracted to his drink. He felt slightly wrong footed. The game was moving quicker than he had anticipated. For a slight moment he had thought he was loosing control. However, a quick reshuffling of the game plan soon corrected that. This was stretching beyond his wildest dreams. She was practically giving herself to him. He had to admit that he didn't like it that much. The fun of the chase was gone and the chasing was one of the prime movers in his games. Now, seemingly, all he had to do was make the final move and take her to bed. At this time he didn't consider that, not only was the game accelerated but it was also twisting in a way that he had never dreamt.

Mike and Peter re-entered the room. The conversation on their arrival was shaped into a discussion about motor bikes. Mike was clearly excited by the intensive week course that lay ahead. So much so that he practically all but ignored Claire. Her face showed disappointment and a longing for real love. As Mike and Peter got more progressively drunk the more they discussed the course or motor cycles. As they spoke Andrew dropped a hand under the table and squeezed Claire's knee, causing her to laugh out aloud.

"What's so funny?" Mike questioned.

"You," Claire replied, "and this stupid conversation. Boys and bikes. To you guys its better than sex isn't it?"

"Well," Peter said, "Bikes and girls go hand in hand. Don't they?"

"Maybe in your world," Andrew said. He squeezed Claire's knee again. "But in the real world I think that most people would disagree."

part two

"Sex and chocolate," Claire said, "that's what does it for me."

"Anyone for chocolate?" Andrew questioned, at which point Claire laughed again.

"Am I missing something?" Queried Mike with a hint of annoyance.

"You're missing it all," Claire replied. "You're missing it all. I'll explain later, much later, if you like?"

THE BOOK OF HURT - Pt4

October 1999

Thursday **21**

They'd found me hanging from a light in my bedroom, carrying out option 'c'. Either I was too late or they were too early, it didn't really matter, I was discovered before my heart had stopped beating. I'd used the belt from my dressing gown as a noose. As far as plans go the carrying out of option 'c' had been pretty damn perfect. Just bad timing was all that had stopped me from freeing my soul from this god-forsaken place. I wish to hell that I had never been found, to be honest. I mean, what favours have they done me? I'm a prisoner both within myself and within this ward. My 'break away', as my doctor had promised, was rapidly turning in a nightmare that not even I could have predicted. Not only are they now pumping me full of drugs but, as a consequence of my pathetic suicide attempt, I was now on what they term as 'status' or, to use their term 'level 2A observation." Basically what this means to me is that I have to have a nurse with me constantly. I can't sleep, eat or bath without a nurse being present. They have to see me 24 hours a day. This, naturally, is fraught with problems. Everybody needs a retreat but, for now, my retreat is a bedroom with a nurse plonked outside a gapping doorway.

part two

There are many disadvantages to this. For me, the prime one is that which is my darker side. So far, no one has paid much attention to the fact that I am 'a cutter'. I harm my self by slicing at my skin with razor blades or, if the mood takes me, by tying a cord around my throat as tightly as I can. Even the cigarette burning is a no go area whilst I am being watched. These things, this darker side, is an essential part of who I am. Without the ability to carry out such actions I remain frustrated. The anti-depressants, the diazepam, none of it stops the desire nor does it, as a result of this need, reduce the anxiety that I feel.

At the moment there is a male nurse camped outside my door, who looks like he's here to stay. He scares me to be honest. He's not the sought of person with whom conversation is an easy thing to achieve. I feel like a criminal and all I've done is express my wishes. I am also having devious thoughts through my lack of harming, thoughts that make me want to do greater harm to myself. The more I contain it the more it swells inside me. I have a razor blade, well hidden, within my room but finding the chance to use is, as I've said, a real hassle. Last night I used it in my bed. My back turned towards my observer I had drawn it back and forth against my skin cutting deeply at my forearms until five, deep cuts were made. Its not the action that counts. Unlike affixation, it is the after events that bring the joy. The blood released by the razor is what matters. The one bad aspect of cutting yourself in such a manner is that blood finds its way onto the bed sheets.

So far, no one has made any comment on the red stains that mark my bed clothes but I'm sure they will when it comes to the changing of the bed linen.

One of the things about being on 2A. for me, is that I feel the need to entertain the nurses. A need to converse with them about matters that for me are of little concern. House, car, pet stuff. I don't care about any of these things. Through such discussions you get to know the nurses too well. After two days I could already list the likes and dislikes of those observing nurses. Such contact leaves me totally confused. I don't want the connection yet, at the time, it is unavoidable not to form some kind of relationship. Relationships remove the nurse and patient divide and in doing so you open yourself up to deeper investigation. giving them deeper insights into yourself. I feel like a puppet. I see the nurses sitting here reading a magazine that is months out of date in a bored fashion and I feel guilty about having them there. So, I feel pressurised into acting. To be the person they want and to keep moving from place to place just to give them input and normality.

I know that this is all my own paranoia and that I am the ill one not them but I just can't stop myself. I think that I care too much about people. Perhaps, it shows how little I care about myself. Either way I am slowly turning into the stereotypical patient. The one good thing about this is that my need to entertain has brought me into contact with the outside areas of my room. I have sat in the smoking room and, even tried the dining area. I don't enjoy it really. I see it more as a punishment for my suicide attempt. Although, I must admit, I get a sense of belonging, of caring and of protection by being on such a high level of observation. Important springs to mind as I write this, although I am also aware that such contact is merely a falsehood.

One question that raises its head is the question of enjoyment. I actually do enjoy these pains placed upon me. Not in terms of belonging or cared for but more a sense of contentment at being at this level in my life. I actually want this pain. I want to dive to the bottom of my emotions just because I can. To feel the moments of despair and to ride them with a child-like, lustful glee. I have even, in one of those moments, tried to explain it to one of the nurses. She'd caught me red-handed, so to speak, a six inch cut across my arm and a razor blade in the other. Afterwards, when all the panic had died down, and the wound washed and dressed, it had been brought up by my current observer.

"Why do you do this?"

"Do what?"

"Hurt yourself. What makes you attempt suicide or the self-harming?"

Why? Umh! I don't know. It just sort of happens."

"But what process makes you do it? These cuts upon your arms," she gestured towards my arms, "Why do it?"

"I'm driven," I explain. "Ah, I don't know. Sometimes I wonder why it is but normally I conclude that, I don't know, that its just the way I am."

"But surely you hurt yourself because you dislike yourself?"

The nurse had left her chair and entered into the bedroom where she sat on the bed. "I'm not sure," I'd replied. "I have never really given any thought to it. I mean, it started at such an early age. I know my consultant, what's his name, you know who I mean. Anyhow, I know he thinks it was the operation I have had but it first happened at seven years old. I mean, how can you put blame on something that is separated by 25 years?"

"Maybe the operation highlighted or invoked something."

"May be it did. I can't be sure of that fact. I can only say it as I feel it." I proceeded to bite at my thumb nail. Chewing it as if it were a mother's nipple.

"But you haven't said anything really about how you feel?"

"Okay, back down! This is a hard one for me. I, umh, now I'm stuck for words. I'm, shit! I'll start again. I began to roll a cigarette. "I hate my body, the shape and the size, its all wrong! I do these things, perhaps, to torture myself because I am myself. Does that make any sense?"

"Yeah, it does but its not really an answer as to why you do it. Hating your body is fine, I understand that but, okay let me propose a question. Do you like your body now more that you did before? You know. Before the cutting and the burning?"

"I don't care. In someways everything is good and there are aspects about me that I enjoy. But this," another gesture to highlight the body, "this is all wrong. Maybe I hurt myself because I don't want the body perfect. I've often thought that I am just on a self-destruct mission and that fucking up my body parts, and my mental parts, is apart of that process. I can't be who I want to be, so I hack at what I can to punish the body and, also, my mind and my self. Does that answer the question?"

"Do you hate yourself that much?"

"Hate," I'd said, "is such a loaded word. I mark my body and my mind not so much as a hate thing but with an enjoyment that comes with it. I'm happiest doing what I do. Now, more than I have ever done so before."

There was a long pause by both of us that was broken by the nurse.

"I don't fully understand this hate and love relationship thing that you have got going on but if you feel that destruction makes you feel happiest I would say that its disclosing in the sense that loving pain is a very complex issue."

"Not really.," I interpreted, "its like a cancer patient knowing that they have 'x' amount of time left. They can either wallow in self-pity or they can live life to the full. I know that I'll kill myself one day soon so I am happy doing the thing I want to do."

"Rather a bleak outlook Melissa, don't you think?"

"No more than anyone else's."

So the conversation had gone on. Spiralling and circling without a solution. As I write this down it seems strange that my conclusion remains one that has no clear-cut definition. Perhaps, it should have. Perhaps just 'being' that which I am is all there needs to be. A 'being' just being. Doing what I want when I want. Okay, so its not all that clean-cut but can I ever be anything. Dear diary, you contain a mixture of my thoughts and happenings and I am possibly likely to change how I feel about who I am and what I do. Such is the contradiction of life. But, for now, its enough to handle within my fucked up little world. I have even given myself a slogan to mutter when I loose track of where I am going. It states;

> free the soul
> eat the flesh

Its something that I feel very strongly about. I'd probably get some sleep were it not for the nurse sitting outside. But, then, to find the salvation I am after requires plenty of thinking time and the best time to think is when you are alone. Well, as alone as one can be under the circumstances.

FLESH OF DREAMS (4)

Now that I have experienced the name 'Andrew' I am full of hope. Within this darkness, this space, I pace like a caged tiger. I am awaiting more information. Hoping to pick up words that I recognise or, more importantly, words that invoke my memory. Recognition of the word 'Andrew' invoked no such memories just the realisation that it was within my vocabulary range. It wasn't like the other word which flashed me images, images of my being. I am pondering a problem. A thought has occurred that makes me wonder why it is that only a few words have filtered through the droning? Are they merely testing me by using such words? No. No, that's paranoia working within me. Who is this 'they''? What do they want with me anyhow? I've so many questions. My mind is awash with them. Maybe 'Andrew' was in the outside world and not within me. God! This is impossible.

I return to the sphere. I understand now what its purpose is and how it can help me. I understand that the dreaming is helping me construct my own reality. But why is it this way? Why am I escorted through these dreams by a girl I do not recognise? More questions than answers. I want to sleep so that I may visit this place again. Learn more insights about myself and the globe. But I cannot control this. Sleep is just something that happens. It comes to me at its own choosing. Fills me with hopes and desires

part two

before the hard smack of reality comes to catch me. I hate this place, this darkness that envelopes me. I want to exist within my dream where I am more real and dimensional. Where I can experience and connect with others. Here, as I am now, I am flat, disjointed and alone. I hate this place. If its not driving me crazy, its that damn noise pulsating through my thoughts. I need to get out of here and, seemingly, I can only do that within my dreams.

I am thinking of the globe again. Pulling up its image from my memory banks with a crystal clear reality. I want it green, brown and blue like hers and I try to change the purple, red and black into a resemblance of her globe. A thought that maybe all one needs is to think, no, to believe with zeal, that it can be changed and it shall be so. So, I try. Changing and challenging the image. Turning its purple into blue and its red into green and I succeed. My globe, at least within my head, is the planet that I want it to be. However, I must heed the warning given to me that closeness is bad. That it may be too soon. That I may see my world before I am born. I retract from the image. She will tell me when it is time to look and I must have patience if this is to succeed.

I refocus upon the drone. The only other thing to have entered my being. Despite its continuation throughout all of this, much to my annoyance, it remains as something little explored by myself. Maybe I need to listen a little harder. To drag it out of the background and bring it to the fore. I follow its rhythmic patterns, as it turns itself on and off, off and on. Yet, there is something else within its pattern. Rhythmic yet free flowing. Its something that I had been unaware of before this time. Then again, apart from earlier, long forgotten times I had paid little attention to how it flowed. It had been more of an annoyance but now, now, well it held an interest for me. It wasn't as I remembered it previously. The drones were not consistent but infrequent and non-linear. There was more of a clarity to its formations that drew me in. Made me want to explore it more. Maybe everything was coming together at last. Me, her, the globe and the drone. It all had a connection, of that I'm sure. I concentrate my focus upon it. Trying to understand it but, as I did so, I fell once more into sleep.

It was the same as always. Nothing seems to changed but then it never did. The room was placed as it was before and, after a moment of retaining its familiarity, the knock on the door came. I knew who it was without looking. She was back and I realised that I held enjoyment at the prospect of seeing her again. Not only was she the lynch-pin to all this but she brought with her a progression. The dream could not move on without her and I wanted to move on. I wanted to explore the globe further. I wanted to see her. I opened the door at the second knock.

"I was beginning to think that you were ignoring me," she exclaimed as she entered.

"No, no, on the contrary. I was merely being reflective."

"Anyone else been here?" There was authority within her tone.

"What? Another teacher you mean?"

"Anybody?" she repeated.

"Nope. Just you as per normal."

"They will come to you though. When they catch the scent of innocent blood. They always do. They'll clamber over one another to reach you and you globe. Your globe is pure and untainted. Easily corruptible and still playable enough for them to re-shape it."

"I know. You warned me last time."

"Just re-emphasising the point. You do still want me teach you, don't you?" It was a question yet it was also a demand. "Trust me."

"Do I have any reason not to?"

"You're asking me? I'm a little bias if I was honest but I believe I am the best."

She sat down upon the sofa, I sat on the one opposite.

the crying shore

"Where is your globe?" She enquired.

I looked at my hands they were empty.

"I don't know."

"Listen. They don't need you just your globe. If you loose it here there can be no other. Always carry it with you. Take the image from your reality and hold onto it as you enter this state. Okay?"

"Okay. But where is it now?"

"Close you eyes," she whispered, "and think about it in your hands."

"You're not going to slap me again are you?"

"Trust is everything. Just do as I ask."

So I did and when my eyes were told to be opened, there is was. Clasped within my cupped hands, my world held by myself. It was still purple, red and black but it had changed. No longer was there a thick, brown gas but lighter more cloud-like casing.

"Its changed!" I said excitedly. "Look, see its changed!"

"But of course it has. I told you all this before. Remember?

part two

You shaped it through your reality. You can not change it here. It will only change within your real world, when you bring it into your thoughts."

"But, I saw it completed within my thoughts!" I exclaimed.

"No, you imagined it completed. There is a difference."

"I don't understand" I said. "What's the difference?"

"You still have so much to learn. Just bring it into your reality and allow it to happen. Don't force it to occur. Anyhow, how are we today?"

"Fine. Should I be anything else?"

"Perhaps not. Would you like to see what lays beyond this room?"

"Take a walk you mean?"

"Well, we could walk but walking is so unnecessary within this place." She opened her arms, extending them fully. "We could walk if you wanted to?"

"How else can I explore the hotel if not..."

"Through my globe. Come. Sit beside me." I moved beside her. "Can you see into the globe?"

"No."

"Look harder, deeper. Focus upon the inside. What do you see?"

I see the hotel as if I were flying over it."

"Good. Now swoop downwards through the roof. What can you see?"

"I see a corridor. There are people in the corridor. People with globes."

"How many people?"

"Six, in total. Two alone and two pairs. One of them is looking at me as if he can see me. Can he?"

"If he is a teacher he will know that your presence is there. Where is your globe."

"In my left hand."

"Good, keep it safe and well protected. Move down the corridor until you get to this room."

I felt myself flowing through the corridor and as I reached it the man who had noticed me began to slow down. I felt compelled to stop above him.

"Do not trust her that looks out for you." He said. "White can be black if you cannot see that it is so. Ask her. Ask her why within this domain she is called the 'Sanity Assassin' and why she stalks alone. Go on. Ask her."

I flowed through the corridor again until I reached my own hotel door and passed through it to where she and I sat upon the sofa.

"I can feel both myself situated here with you and myself looking on," I said.

"Does it help you understand how the globe works a little clearer? She enquired.

Oh yes! I can understand now what it is that I must do once my own globe is complete. However..."

"There are questions?"

"Two to be precise. May I ask them?"

"I am your teacher. How can I teach without questions?"

"Okay, good. The first questions is how can I use what I have experienced here to bring me back into the real world?"

"A fair question. It was one that I was hoping to avoid for now. Alas, now is as good a time as any. You said yourself that you experienced yourself both sitting here and flowing above. If the two have touched they would have become one being."

"So, I could have tasted reality then?"

"No, not then. In your globe, at the right time, that is when. Not before nor through someone else's globe. Touching yourself within my planet would only have left you here. This place would have become your reality."

"I don't fully understand," I said.

"You will soon enough. And the other question?" She puzzled.

"Why do they call you the 'Sanity Assassin'?"

"Who told you that!" She was angry. "What else did they tell you? Tell me."

"Nothing else. Just that."

"I told you not to trust others and you have chosen to ignore my advice." Her aggressive tones were becoming sharper.

part two

Without any warning, she reached across and, with her globe holding hand, smashed it against the side of my face.

I awoke.

THE MASTER OF GAMES – IV

The phone twice rang and Andrew answered.

"Hello."

"Hi!"

"Who's this?"

"Who do you think?"

"Claire, hi. Sorry I didn't recognise the voice."

"No problem. I just phoned to let you know that Mike has finally gone. I thought he would never leave. He was full of 'love you' and 'miss you' shit. Anyhow, he's gone now and for one whole week."

"Do you feel better?" quizzed Andrew

"I feel bloody great to be honest. Like, like someone has climbed off my back. Know what I mean?"

"Not really."

"I feel like I have space, the ability to move around at my leisure. I have free will and can do what I damn well want."

part two

"That's good," Andrew said. "See, I told you it would make you feel better, didn't I? So, why are you phoning?"

"Just to check that you were still coming over to stay. That's all. That and I needed to tell someone, no you, how I feel"

"You find all this space, which you seem to enjoy, and you still want me to fill it?"

"Yeah, sure. Why not? At least you and I can have some fun together."

"You make it sound sordid!"

"I think that's just you dreaming," she said. "I'm talking about going out to places. Places that Mike refused to go to. I know you, you're game for most things."

"Am I now?"

"Yeah, I think so. Don't tell me that you're not up for a little excitement this week. You are still coming over. Aren't you?"

"Oh yeah. I want to see what a 'Mike-free' Claire looks like. So, what do you have in mind?"

"I don't know. Something crazy. Something that we don't normally do. Something that has a good memory. You know, something shared and happy that only we can share."

"Are you sure that you're not trying to get me into bed?" Quizzical laugh.

"Bed is boring. I want more than that. Much more."

"Okay. Look, I've got a few things to sort out here, which will take me a couple of hours, then I need to pack a bag and shit and then I'll be over. Okay?"

"No! Come now!" Claire screamed.

"I'll be there by 1 o'clock. That's the best I can offer. Why don't you use the time to think about doing things? Roll a joint, relax."

"Okay, okay. But be here soon."

"As soon as I can"

"Excellent! See you later."

"Goodbye."

Andrew replaced the phone upon the table. He was unsure why but there was something out of the ordinary going on and it bothered him. He thought about the simplicity. The fact that this was too easy. She was giving herself to him. Perhaps he shouldn't have been bothered. Maybe she'd just dropped into the trap of falling for his charms and graces. But it was too easy. It made him, if Andrew has been honest, scared of taking her bait. That was it! It was her bait that he was taking not the other way around. His fear was her game. He turned it over and over within himself. Looking at the different permutations, the possible outcomes, who was doing what and why. Then a thought occurred to him. He knew her game, wasn't quite sure of the specifics, but he knew. He realised that such an acknowledgement held power. That the game, such as it was, was back under his control because of this realisation. Andrew smiled. A game within a game was something else. It was a challenge that excited him. He would play it 'her' way, as far as she was aware but he would play it to his rules. He climbed off the chair with anticipation rampant within his body and began to pack the things he required.

It was actually half past one when he arrived. He was purposefully late. It demonstrated that he was in control of his actions, not her. She wouldn't like it but, hey, what the hell. This was, seemingly, a battle of wills and it had to fought with close precision if he was to become the winner. He had considered the fact that, in the end, they both seemed to be after the same goal but, after further thought, he had realised that even if they were after the same outcome someone had to be the loser. A loser was something he couldn't possibly be. This was, after all, his game.

She answered the door. He could sense her annoyance at his lateness but she still beamed a welcoming grin and an all-embracing hug.

"Hi Ya!" They both backed away.

"Hi, sorry I'm late. I, er, had a lot of things to do before hand. Thought it better to get them out of the way in order to keep the week a bit free."

"Great. Its not a problem. You're always late anyhow." It was true. He was always late. Sometimes on purpose but sometimes not. Either way he was always late. Claire was, however, annoyed of that Andrew had no doubt.

"Any chance of some tea?" He questioned as he crossed over the threshold and deposited his bags upon the floor.

"You know where it is."

"I thought you were being my slave for the week?"

"Did I say that?"

"Pretty much. That's the deal isn't it?" Andrew laughed.

"I'm more a mistress than a slave but I'll bow to you this once. Just don't expect it all the time."

"Fine," Andrew said, sitting at the dinning room table. "Where's Carey?" He shouted through to the kitchen.

"Carey? Oh, Yeah. She's working and then going out for dinner with some guy from work. She said she had a hot date so I expect that means she won't be back for a couple of days. Dirty stop-out. You know Carey, never lost the hippy thing. So, it'll just be you and I for dinner. I don't know what you want?"

"How's about I eat you and you eat me?" Andrew said.

"What? Sorry. I didn't hear what you said over the kettle boiling", said Claire entering the room.

"I said anything, as long as there is no meat."

"You know I'm vegetarian"

"Oh yeah. Sorry, I forgot."

She disappeared again and re-appeared carrying two mugs.

"Here's your tea," she said placing a cup in front of him.

"Thanks. You're looking better already."

"Yeah. I feel it. Relaxed and chilled basically."

"So, what you got planned? I bet you haven't given it any thought."

"Oh yes I have! I've got a few ideas to fling at you. See what you think."

Four hours later they were eating dinner. They'd settled for Chinese, a take-away, seeing as neither one of them could be bothered to cook. Andrew paid and Claire washed the dishes. Dinner, as it always was, was followed by cards. Halfway through the scores were fairly even, with Claire just ahead. It was a dragging game that absorbed time slowly. Both parties were seemingly growing tired of it.

"This game need a little spicing up, don't you think?" Andrew enquired as he lay down a card.

"In what way?"

"I dunno. Loser has to do a forfeit perhaps?"

"Like what?"

"Loser makes the winner breakfast or something."

Yeah, okay. I'm game for that seeing as I've nearly won."

"Deal?"

"Deal." They shook hands on it and continued to play. A few hands later Andrew turned around to Claire and asked,

"So, what's your deal, if you win?"

"Umh! All the trimmings and I get to see you in that apron that Mike bought me."

"Just the apron?"

"That's negotiable," Claire replied. "And if you win?"

"Well, breakfast obviously. Not so into the apron thing. I think I'd prefer a topless waitress bringing me breakfast."

"You are joking!"

"Let's just see who wins, okay? But, no backing out."

"Fine. Give it your best shot."

A hour later, at around midnight, the game drew to a close. Claire protested but there was little point. Andrew had won and that was the simple fact of it all.

"So what do you want?"

"At the moment I'd like a joint." He began to roll one whilst sitting upon the floor.

"No, I mean..."

"I know what you mean! I'm just making you sweat a little, that's all. I could put you out of your misery but I think I'll wait until I've finished this," he said gesturing at the joint.

"Tell me now!" Claire demanded.

"Make some tea and I may lessen my desire."

"No way! Just tell me."

"I already have," Andrew smiled.

"I thought you were joking." Claire winced.

"I never joke about topless breakfasts."

"No! no way. Never, ever, ever."

"A deal is a deal," he reminded her.

"I'll think about it but I'm not going to promise anything."

"All right. But, if you don't do it then, I'm afraid, you have to do another forfeit of my choosing."

"Like what?"

"Oh, I don't know but I'm sure that I'm twisted and sick enough to come up with something awful for you to do."

"You bastard!" She laughed.

"You'd better believe it honey. Now, what about that cup of tea?"

THE BOOK OF HURT – Pt5

October 1999

Tuesday 26

Wow! A lot has happened since I last wrote in this diary. So much so that I don't know where to start. I guess at the beginning would be as good a place as any, but what beginning do I start at? Okay, here goes the roller-coaster.

I'm now off 2A observation. Apparently, I was enjoying it too much, and that I was viewing as a privilege instead of a punishment. I mean, enjoying it is hardly what I'd have called but I must confess that I felt suddenly isolated when I was taken off it. I even cried. Anyhow, the status was dropped two days ago along with belts, leads and other assorted long implements which, rather stupidly I think, included the headphones for my personal stereo. So, now I am stuck without music. I guess, in a way, I asked for it happen so I got what I deserved. As a consequence of my being unable to entertain myself within my own space I have been forced to venture out off my room and into the lion's den. I'm easy prey for these people and I can feel them knawing at my bones. They introduce themselves and then they dump their shit onto me. Telling me what's wrong with them, why they hate their doctors, why they feel like they do, why they are not getting the help they deserve. You name it I've heard it. There are some very strange people in here but they, as I, have an illness and thus, I suppose, can not be held responsible for their ways. Regardless, I'm easy prey. The strange thing is that they never enquire as to my presence, such is their own self-absorbency, and I'm glad for it. The gossip line in this place meant that everybody knew why I was on 'status' and, in some twisted way, this has meant that I have gained some position amongst them. Proved myself as it were. I am now worthy to walk within these walls that are bounced off by drugged-out patients going in no fixed direction.

One of the things about my 'outing', as it were, is that I had teamed up with a man called 'Ian'. Ian is Scottish and has a tendency towards suicide. Maybe that's why I like him. Talking to him has taught me a lot about the 'how' and 'whys' of killing yourself. We've already spent days planning our deaths together. Weighing up the benefits of hanging as oppose to overdose or discussing what pills go best with other pills. It had become a team effort. Ian had plumped for a hand full of sleeping pills and then, once slipping into sleep, hanging himself from an oak tree that lies just outside. I must confess I found this method a touch over dramatic and clearly seeking attention.

We went together to get the pills. Went up to the hospital pharmacy and got them with no questions asked. We'd split the pills down the middle and retreated in to our own private spaces for quiet contemplation. As for myself, I'd planned a more subtle attempt. All I did was to collect a few real pills given out by the ward. 'Palming off' is the name for it. I've been palming for a few days and had amounted a small collection that has been enhanced by those bought by our trip to the pharmacy.

Ian was the first to go. I'd had a feeling, as he announced it to me, that his effort would be ineffective. He'd had an air about him that suggested it was more for effect rather than cause. He'd taken the pills, I'd bumped into him in a corridor, a big smile across his face and I wished him 'luck' in his venture and then he was gone. As I'd entered my bedroom I'd preyed for his victory but only half-heartedly and had laid my head down to sleep for a few hours.

Four hours later I was awoken for dinner, or supper as they call it here. I braved the dining room partly because I was hungry but more so because I was curious to see if Ian was there or not. The food was shit but then hospital food usually is. As I'd entered the room I'd scanned it nervously. Ian wasn't there. I sat at a table facing the door anxiously awaiting and remained throughout dinner, but still he didn't show. I left most of the food. I found it hard to eat whilst also thinking of a dead person hanging from something, somewhere.

part two

After dinner I'd walked down the corridor that allowed for observations on the oak tree to be carried out. I'd felt both a sense of relief and disappointment at not seeing him there. I was relieved due to the increased possibility of his being alive and disappointed that, seemingly, he had failed to carry out his thoughts. I turned around in the corridor and made my way back towards the main area. As I'd approached halfway a side door, one of the interview rooms, opened and Ian, tearful and head down, exited. He had turned away from me, failing to notice my presence, and had headed to the main area also.

I'd called his name, "Ian, Ian" but he'd made no attempt to turn around. I'd quickened my pace and caught up with him just as he reached the main room.

"Hey," I'd said, tapping him on the shoulder. "What happened? Why were you in the interview room?"

"They found me. They fucking found me! I'd taken the pills and was doing the bed-sheet when they fucking found me!"

"So, what did they do?"

"They forced me to tell them what I was doing."

"And me?" I'd said.

"I didn't mention you. They did because we've talked so much at the moment. They asked if you knew, if you'd planned anything."

"And?"

"I didn't tell them anything about you. I just said that we talked. I didn't say what about just that we'd talked."

"So, what are they going to do?"

"Send me back to fucking Glasgow on the first train tomorrow. They said they couldn't cope with me here so I'm off"

At this point he entered into the main room and the conversation stopped. I'd made my way towards my room in order to check that my stash was safe. I'd passed the nurse, himself coming out of the interview room, that had dealt with Ian but he didn't say anything as I sped passed. Entering the room filled me with panic. Where could you hide 50 pills? Every place I'd thought off seemed too obvious and then, slowly, it dawned on me. I'd cut a hollow into the curtain seem and began to insert the pills as quickly as possible. I'd placed the last pill and straightened the curtain when there was a knock upon my door. It had been him, the nurse.

"I've been talking to Ian," he'd said, "do you have anything to tell me?"

"About what?" I'd asked.

"About storing tablets perhaps."

"Is that, er, what Ian told you?"

"That's irrelevant. Do you have any pills?"

"No," I'd answered flatly.

"I'm placing trust here," he'd said.

"So believe my story then."

"Okay, if you say so then I'll assume this discussion is closed." He had got up and left. I felt bad about lying, still do, but it made me decide to wait a few days before taking them.

Those few days have now passed by. For some reason tonight is the night. I got to say farewell to Ian and wish him the best and I'm sad now that he has gone. I'm nervous as I am about to attempt my second suicide attempt within this ward. It feels strange. Alone within the quietness of this room. It almost feels surreal in a way. I may as well have been on film as I removed the stitching from the curtain, thread by thread, to reveal my treasure. Now, there rests a little mound of pills upon my bedroom floor. They say "eat me" but I'm afraid to do so. I am just sitting here writing this and staring at the pills which, occasionally, I run my hands through. I have no real heavy thoughts, just a desire to do it that mixes itself with the fear to generate an uneasy feeling.

I have decided to write and take the pills in between thoughts and sentences. It seems more natural that way. So, that is what I am doing. 8 down 42 to go. I am thinking of Ian. Wondering if he was ever part of the club, as it were. Did he really want to do it? Death is easy to achieve. It is all around us, hand upon each one of our shoulders. 20 pills down. Surely, if someone wanted to do it then they would. A knife to slice a vein. A piece of glass to cut a throat. Death is everywhere. I can feel it coming to me. Not physically but mentally. The pills are dropping faster now. There is an urgency in what I do. I don't want to pass out until I have taken them all. I also don't wish to consider what and why I am doing this. All those people I leave behind. What about them? I don't like these thoughts. Stop!

I have taken all 50 pills now. I feel the effects upon my body, my irrational thoughts. I want to end this by saying that I have freed my soul and killed the flesh. I only hope that this is true. Goodbye.

TO HELL WITH UNCERTAINTY [d]

The mirrors were back. One at the front of him, the other behind. He was back naked before them with the usual glee. Already, he was absorbed within the mirrored image of self. The reflection that allowed himself to move away from the real world and into his world of fantasy. He liked it that way. The threesomes, the virgin sex, these had their place but they always involved him presenting himself as that which he was. The reflection was different. Abstracted, distant and, to him, somebody else.

This time he was standing with his right hand grasping an already fully erect penis, which he was caressing softly and with care. He already felt light-headed from the prospect of the act of affixation. He liked to see it. See it reflected back at himself. That never failed to maximise his arousal. So, here he stood. Right hand wanking whilst the left hand grasped at the noose that had been tied around one of the visible beams within his bedroom. He looked at himself and the twisted old piece of hemp rope that lay to one side of his head. Left hand fingering the noose, he stepped up on to the wooden box placed at his feet.

"This time you die," he sneered. "No fucking more reality, just death, you shit, slow and sure" With his left hand firmly grasping, he drew his head forward and up into the rounded rope. His gaze remained upon the image in front of him. The rope was a loose fit but then it always was. Affixation via this method was a dangerous game to play. The length of the rope, and the noose it had made, were marked in places with a series of lines. These lines were life saving and important. They insured that once the box had been tipped forward he could, when he wanted to, re-step upon it to ensure his life. A few inches one way and he would fail to hang, a few the other way and he would die for certain. The uncertainty that this brought merely heightened his pleasure. He knew that he was playing a game, a game that few would understand, but he also knew the realities of such games.

Once, a few years ago now, his method had been different. He would tie the rope over the top of the door and affixiate by allowing his knees to buckle from underneath him. This one time it had all gone wrong. As he had allowed his legs to buckle he had slipped sideways and banged his head against a wall. It hadn't rendered him unconscious but it had made the rope tighten by a far greater extent than normal. It hadn't been helped by his naivity at the time and, subsequently, he had panicked. Clutching at the rope with a wild desperation. With hindsight he realised that his panic stricken, flaying body had served him more harm than good. But then not everyone has that ability, nor the experience that allowed him this insight now.

Now? Now he was wiser. He had learnt the tricks and safety measures. There was still an element of risk but

part two

these elements were part of the process. Now? Now he was standing upon a box readying himself to tip it over with his feet. Some people think that it is the actual affixation, the hanging, that is the joy but, especially for him, it was this moment that brought the most pleasure with it. The edge of actually doing it. The seconds of doubt, of fear and anxiety and the expectation of things to come. It was this time that gave him the buzz. He revelled in it. He looked into the mirror more intently. He could see the fear and the excitement within his eyes. Desperate yet not dispairing. Seeking a pleasure that, more likely than not none would ever share. It was a powerful time. A time that only he controlled. No other could affect him. The balance hung within his hands.

With his right hand still conveying this time to his penis, he gazed one final time at the image in front of him. He felt the need to release his seed. It was something he rarely did when affixiating, as if he didn't want to lessen the moment. He positioned his feet onto the box's edge, eyes never leaving the image. His left hand lightly fingered the hemp. His eyes widened. His feet began to rock the box. His right hand worked himself harder. The box rocked further. His left hand held the hemp tighter. His eyes displayed fear and anticipation. His body grew rigid. The box rocked one final time. His mind froze. His eyes lied. The box flipped. His left hand gripped tightly at the rope as the box over turned and then relaxed. His feet were merely inches away from the floor and yet, he felt the call of death. He also felt the breath being drawn out of him as he swung freely, feeling the threat of unconsciousness and a certain end. The reflection that stared back at him was like a painting. Within such despair was a point of beauty. A poetic image that spoke little but said it all. It spoke of inner pains, unimagined, of a past tainted with harm and of how pathetic a human could actually become. It was a scene with many facets.

He felt himself cum. Its rush merged with the rush of affixation. He heard it within his pounding ears. He watched it splatter across the mirror, lost in a world where life and death danced as partners. Then it became a game of choice, as it always was at this point. He could continue to hang, to call in death, or he could reach out to the safety of the box. He could flip either way but he opted for life in the end. His feet began to search for the box and its safety. Planting his feet upon its solid form. He relaxed as he touched it with a certainty. Taking a few moments to recapture his composure, eyes closed. With eyes still closed he began to remove the noose. He always did it that way. The image too haunting to face as a reality. Only when the noose was off did he open his eyes to the image in front of himself. A ring of red hung around his neck, which he gazed at as he stepped off the box.

When it was all over and cleaned away he felt better. Despite enjoying the act of affixation, the image, after orgasm, never failed to shock and disgust him. In fact, when he thought about it, it all disgusted him. He disgusted himself and brought others into his acts as well perhaps, just to make him feel better. Perhaps, but at this point he didn't give it any thought. He merely laid upon the bed and tired to reflect upon a time when he was, to use a word only he understood, normal and not deviant.

THE THIRD MOVEMENT OF LIFE AND DISGUISE

the light in dead of night
helps - serves - to protect
in times I cry out
to - you -follow
the faith - the land
a hand of peace
ready to guide
can you hear it
the force
the light - the night
the scent of life
limbo - I feel
alive as you are
I say nothing
but hope in days
dies - hard - fast rules
that cross an open mind
touch nerves - wake
find - I feel
no sense - sense
life without sorrow
a smile - a touch
I walk towards an age
I dance - you dance
I feel - steal - night
light arrows pierce me

part two

cry - tears - hope
swallow the tiny thoughts
of us - you - are they
anyone or everyone
deep in thought
I cradle my knees
a light arrow pierces my heart
touches me - life
I love - I touch
you
but nothing can grow
I sense - sense
the scent - sense
my mind - creeps
open - it slides
and people - stone
stand alone
I swallow - I feel
nothing - life
takes over to need
I run - braced into the wind
the night time closes my eyes
I loose - my soul - my disguise
I am a being
I cry - laugh - and then I die

part three

"dancing the dance
where fire grows"

SLICE - MY LIFE

slice - knife
into flesh
causing pain - yet happiness
satisfied - with angel grin
knowing that it has always been
circular movements - constant time
smearing blood through battered lines
slice - knife
creating life
cuts like a razor through the strife
self inflicted - contradicted
words that flow - thick as snow
yet, somewhere deep behind
the sharpened knife will always find
your deepest and your darkest fears
cutting through the outer tears
slice - knife - this is my life
carved up - razored - neatly diced
channels formed by sharpest blade
tainted with hurt - the carving made
mark to the deepest - towards the soul
leaving you shallow - not quite whole

FLESH OF DREAMS (5)

"That hurt," I said as I opened the doorway for the Sanity Assassin to enter.

"Sorry. I was angry. Perhaps without true cause. There are many people here with many names, as I told you before. They call me the Sanity Assassin out of jealousy, that is all. The teachers, those others, envy my skills at guidance. I get people to form their globes quicker and more complete than any other. It is, however, a name that I despise so, if you'd please, refrain from using it. If that's okay?

"I rather liked it."

"Forget it or this teaching is off!"

"Okay, Okay, but what do I call you?"

"Here I am Tiko, if you remember. That name suits me fine."

"Tiko it is then," I said, "just don't hit me like that again."

"I won't if I can help it."

"So, what are we doing today," I asked without consideration.

"Allow me to look at your globe," she said.

I passed it over to her. It had, I noticed as I donated it, changed a little bit more. Progressed further.

"I see that it has been working well for you. Your time here, if this continues, will be, I think, rather shorter than most others."

"Really?" Excitement pulsed through my blood.

"Why do you keep questioning me? If I am to teach you then you must trust what I say. We have this conversation time and time again, yet you still pursue it despite my answers."

"I'm sorry." She was clearly annoyed and defensive about her position. I wasn't sure why. There was a change about her that was hard to place. Calling her the 'assassin' had obviously opened up old wounds. I was curious about this. Surely, someone who had as much belief in their abilities, such as she, would have merely laughed off this name calling. Yet, such was her rage that she had smacked me with her globe. This opened up many questions., but, now was not the time to explore them. She broke my thought.

"Today, we shall enter into your globe. We shall do this together but remember not to touch anything or no one, regardless of who they are. Okay?" My curiosity was replaced by excitement.

"My globe? Are you sure that...." She held up her hand. I understood immediately that she did not want the question.

"Here," she said handing back the globe, "take hold of it."

I retrieved it in to out-stretched, cupped hands.

"Now look into it. Allow it to become as much a part of you as you are to it. Sink into it. Believe in it. Can you pass through the outside? Through the glass?"

I ran my thumbs over the surface. It rippled as I did so as if liquid in form. As I did I felt myself enter into its atmosphere. Tiko was already there. Circling the poisoned skies like a bird. She reached out her right hand and grabbed at my arm as I drifted past. We circled together. Gliding through dense clouds until the ground below was visible. I saw many things that had gone unnoticed before. The dark lands were broken sporadically with green. The hills, still red with lava flow, were cooling to allow growth to occur. The waters, which looked dark and black from the outside were, in fact, dark blue and green. Algae was growing upon it. It was alive. I felt elated to see my planet this way. We circled the seas and followed the shore line before heading further out to sea.

"I want to show you this." she said.

I waited and saw. Saw something move within the water. We followed it along its chosen path.

"What is it?" I asked.

"Life."

My elation turned into manic excitement.

"From these things you were born. From the algae, this fish like creature. from this you were born," she repeated.

"Can we look? Under the water! Can we look?"

"Of course. Remember, however, not to touch anything that is alive." With this we plummeted through the skies and glided into the water. Side by side we followed the creature for several minutes before, much to my annoyance, I was yanked upwards and away from the sea.

"Why?"

"The algae. It is life also You cannot touch it. I think that it is time to leave here."

"I don't want to! I want to see more."

part three

"Soon you will. Soon the globe will be your home, but not yet, not now."

We retreated back into the hotel room.

" I am sure that you have many questions to ask about this journey. However, do not ask them now. Next time we meet I will answer all that you ask but not now. Now is a time for contemplation. You have entered your world and seen it as it grows. For now, that is enough. I would like you to consider carefully what has happened here. Consider it carefully before you ask your questions."

"If you wish," I replied.

"I insist. Oh! And please do not try to enter the globe by yourself. You still have much to learn. The globe was already challenged by your encounter with the algae and, I'm sure, that you see yourself with a better sense of self than that?"

"Can I ask one question Tiko?"

"Just one."

"You are a woman but what am I? I haven't seen a mirror or a reflection of myself. What am I?"

"Oh, you are many things, many genders. I too am woman and man. I am multi-dimensional as gender goes. You? Well, you have a true gender, on the outside world, but here you are neutral. Neither and yet both. Allow yourself to acknowledge this. I must go, which means that you must go also."

"I understand," I said. "Please don't hurt me too hard this time."

"I promise."

Slap. I am awoken again,

A moment passes before the drone enters into my head. I focus upon the noise for a while. Its rhythmic beat definitely changes. Maybe it is trying to talk to me now? I remain confused by the connection of the parts of my being and, I'm unsure why, but something happened in my last dream that made me feel unclear and insecure. Something that, if I have any, I can not put my finger on. It has something to do with the now and the then. A statement made, an image. I'll keep searching until I nail it. But, it definitely was a connection. A chance to salvage some form of sanity. To fill this head space with a little hope.

In terms of the droning noise I must confess to finding it more comfortable now. Perhaps it took me over the edge and I am now insane with it as my torturer. I like it because, perhaps not on purpose, it gave me something I could relate to. Up to this time I have heard the name "Andrew" over ten times. So, why haven't they said the other name, the name that I want? I must ask Tiko about this next time I see her. Maybe she knows the name. Would she tell me if she did? Her recent attitude towards questions of any kind makes me scared to ask them.

This connection. The globe, flying, touching water, seeing life. Life! That is what bugs me. The Sanity assassin had said many things about the globe but nothing about my reality, my place here and now. Is seeing it within the globe the same as being here? My globe involves, clearly, evolution. How can my globe evolve precisely to this place? Again, I am merely asking questions. She did say that this globe would release me from this darkness, didn't she? I am not quiet yet sure as to how and why.

I think about this question and, as I do, a realisation takes hold. The Sanity Assassin is drawing me inward not outward. She is drawing me into her world, not my own. I feel cheated at this for, despite desiring to be whole again, I do not wish to be so in a controlled world. Who looks after the globes once they have been entered? I need to remember these questions, they hold importance and fragments of realisation. How do I get out of this assuming that the globe road is a false one? Is it the drone that holds the key? It has changed as far as my memory can recall. Perhaps I should reach out to it somehow and allow it touch me.

I push my thoughts, hoping to hear. Push myself until my mind holds nothing else. I am calling the name given to me, "Andrew," as loud as I can. I try not to waver in my dedication. If I have a voice then it is screaming. Screaming so loud that nothing else could be heard. Time slips by yet I continue my calling despite my tiredness. Continued and continued until I thought I would burst open from the inside. Still I pursued it. Believed it with faith. A faith that allowed access to nothing else.

Then it came. The word that I had been waiting so long for. A name that filled my head with images, of childhood, of growing up, family and with hope. I understood only three words, "Melissa, shut up" and that was all. But, to me, it was like being born again. I had made contact with the outside and remembered the name. I repeated it to myself until I realised that I had allowed the images to fade away into fragments. It didn't matter, I had broken through at last and, yet, although the name excited me, I failed to see any connection between 'Andrew', 'Melissa' and me. True, it seemed, by the sentence, that I was 'Melissa' but I couldn't be sure of that with any great certainty.

THE BOOK OF HURT - Pt 6

October 1999

Saturday 30

I'm still writing so I need not tell you that things did not go as intended. I feel as if I have failed my test. Days ago I criticised Ian for not really belonging to 'the club' and now I am no longer a member either. I can't remember who or what saved me exactly. I recall certain things happening but not enough to finish the painting. What do I remember? I recall taking the pills, of being dragged from the floor to a seat and from the seat into the corridor where two nurses, one on each arm, dragged me back and forth. I have a hazy recollection of being put into an ambulance, but no idea how I got there. I have a faint image of being in causality. Of me lying on a trolley bed and of a vast collection of people doing things to me. Shining lights into eyes, blood pressure, injections and intravenous drips. After that all I can recall is entering into the Acute Medical Unit ward.

After that two days passed before I regained consciousness. It was four o'clock in the morning and I freaked out at the tubes and machines that were attached to me. I felt like an android. These machines constantly checking my status, keeping me alive. I remember getting out of bed with little, or no, regard of the equipment that surrounded me. As I swung my legs off the bed and onto the floor the alarms had started. I'd panicked at all the different bleeps and sirens and had hurried to my feet to flee the noise and confusion. I made it into the ward corridor where I stood screaming.

"Where the fuck am I? What day is it? Help me!"

I was crying, confused and afraid. Two nurses came towards me but I don't recall what they said. Each took an arm and turned me around to head back into my room.

"Where am I?"

"You're in hospital. Do you recall how you got here?"

"What day is it?"

"Its Friday. You've been a sleep for a few days. Do you remember how you got here?"

We entered into the room I had awoken in.

"Here, lie down." So I did.

They began to reinsert the mechanical devices into me.

"You took an overdose. You are in the Acute Medical Unit and you were brought here from A & E."

part three

"But, how do.."

"No more talking," said one of the nurses. "Try to rest and a doctor will see you in the morning. Okay?"

"Okay," I said sleepily.

I fell to sleep. When I awoke I was aware that some of the machines had gone. I must have been considered 'better' under their terms. I remember just feeling like shit. I was also, at that point, realising that it had been a failure. I didn't want to be here, I had hoped for death. But no. I was still very much alive, just hung over from the pills. I laid in quite contemplation. I knew that I would have to return to the psychiatric ward and I was afraid of their reaction. As it happens there was no great fuss. Later, in the morning, the doctor had come and concluded that I was well enough to leave. As soon as I'd got dressed a man entered my room and announced that he was to escort me back to my room.

Nobody had said anything as I pushed open the door leading into the ward. They had just stopped and stared. Staff and patients alike. My 'named nurse' was there, still looking efficient as she browsed through someone's case notes. Finally she looked away from her notes and at me.

"Go down to your room Melissa, we'll talk down there."

It was a command more than a suggestion and so I set off to my bedroom. Ten minutes later she emerged. I was lying upon the bed, she sat upon the chair. She scares me, I've decided. Her ways are blunt and to the heart. The conversation was started by her.

"So, what was that all about?"

"How do you mean?"

"Why do it? Why do it here?"

"Perhaps I wanted to kill myself." She scoffed at this.

"So why did you do it where you knew you would be found. You're on observation every half an hour so you must have known you'd be found before anything serious happened."

"I, er, didn't think about it in that way. I just wanted to do it."

"Don't you think that its stupid?"

I got the gist of her comments straight away and knew what she was implying.

"You think that this is all a game don't you?

"I never said that," she replied.

"You didn't have to, I can read in between the lines."

"Well? Was it a game?" She seemed uninterested.

"No!" I said flatly. "I wanted to do it. That's why I did it, to end my life."

"You knew you would be found."

"Yeah sure. By then I was hoping it would be too late to do anything for me."

She scoffed again. "I see something different than you. You see," she sat forward. "What you did was attract attention. I see what you did as a way of seeking attention. Correct me if I'm wrong."

"I don't want to talk about it anymore. I'm tired and pissed-off at your suggestion." I waved her away with my hand. "I'll talk later."

"The doctor will want to see you." She said as she got up. "Okay?"

"Yeah,. Yeah, whatever." I lay my head upon the pillow as she left. A minute later I was calling myself everything under the sun. Even worse. I was beginning to see sense in what she'd been saying. Maybe I was just playing this.

Anyhow, a few hours later and I am summoned to see my doctor. I was nervous again, wondering how he'd take it and what he would make of it. I was scared of him at the best of times. I'd felt like a school girl sent to see the head-mistress as I made my way down the corridor towards the interview rooms. I reached the door and rapped my knuckles against it.

"Come in."

Nervously I pulled down the handle and the door began to open. Eventually it was open enough to walk through but its openness also allowed for me to see him sitting there behind his desk, touching certain notes within a file and, occasionally, writing something down.

"Come in, sit down. I'll be with you in a second."

"Thanks." Fear and anxiety flowed through me. I began to fidget. Eventually he closed the folder and put inside a briefcase. He looked up at me.

"I don't know what more we can do for you. This has been you second attempt in as many weeks, has it not?"

I nodded.

"You cut yourself and, seemingly, have little regard for life. You know my opinion on this already. The surgery has left a pretty sizeable mental scar. This ward seems merely to re-enforce you rather than help you. You seem reluctant to help yourself, which is called for, especially for a self harmer. Only you can stop it. Do you want to stop?"

"I just want to end it all," I cried. "I'm fed up with this whole, erm, fucking life. Is it too much to ask?"

"Whilst you are on this ward, yes it is too much to ask. We have a responsibility to keep you safe. Seemingly, you are unwilling to accept this help. We have staff here to talk to you and for you to tell them how you feel. You seem to use neither. I'm really at a loss as to what I, we as a ward, can do for you without your co-operation and dedication. If something isn't done then I think, in a few months, you will be dead. I believe that you just need to come to terms with the surgery. Yet, to get at this we need to go through a series of games that involve different types of self-harm. Wouldn't you agree?"

"Not entirely. You see the focus of my problems to be the surgery. Maybe it is, I don't know. But, if it is, then it has more to do with the finality of if. If you know what I mean? I don't regret the surgery but I am willing to admit that it has opened up channels or broken barriers that I held mentally. I need to re-learn how to cope. How to reconstruct these broken barriers."

"Umh! Do you think you are doing that?"

"I've started," I said annoyed.

"Started by two attempted suicides and a total misuse of our facilities. As I said. at the beginning, I'm not sure that we can help you through this. Being on the ward merely enhances your behaviour. I know that there is a likelihood that you have a blade of some description hidden somewhere and I'm sure you will use it. Will you tell me about that then?"

"Okay. So I do have a razor for emergencies. I'm not going to tell you where it is however because I don't want to loose it."

"More games," the doctor sighed. "You see, this is my point. We are here to help you. This is not a prison but a medical ward for people to step back a little and reorganise themselves. It is to help people deal with problems. Yet, this is clearly not how you see it."

"I don't know what I see anymore. I came here to get away from some problems I'd had and I end up like this." I shrugged. "I feel I'm getting worse, not better. You know what I mean?"

"I think that the time has come," said the doctor relaxing into the back of his chair, "where it is more dangerous

part three

for you to stay here upon the ward. I predict that once off this ward, with the exception of several A & E visits, you will return to normal. What do you say about that?"

"I came here for a couple of weeks rest and now I'm this"

"Precisely! This is why, well one of the reasons to be honest, we would like to see you leave the ward before it gets too late to help you."

"You mean, you're going to discharge me?"

"It would be for the best."

"But, you haven't done anything for me. Once outside I'll still feel as I did when I came here. The only difference is that I am now taking serious drugs which have, I reckon, only made me worse. Tell me what the fuck you have done for me? For my inner turmoil?"

"We've done everything we can. That's all I can say. How can we help you if you don't help yourself? We could keep a 24 hour watch upon you but even that turned into a game for you. Sneaking around, cutting yourself without the nurses finding out. All the ward is to you is a game board. You feel that whilst here you must win. But, there's nothing to win. We are not players, only you are a player and we can't stop you playing. Don't you think?"

"I don't know. I've already said everything I can about my position. I'm ill, mentally, and seemingly in need of help. Even if these are games the, oh shit! what's the word, doesn't matter. Even if these are games there must be something underlying this?"

"I don't doubt that for a second. Attention seekers always have hidden agendas. But what can we do to access it?

"Talk to me," I blurted.

"Look. You won't go to any other hospital and after 2 weeks nothing has changed for you here. How can we help you?

The doctor sighed deeply and picked up a pencil from his desk. He began to twirl it every so often.

"Once the medication has taken effect then I'm sure you will see all this in a different light. Apart from the medication the remaining stuff is up to you. If you want to release the barriers only you and outside helpers can achieve this. We can do nothing more here."

"So, I'm discharged then?"

"As from the end of the day, yes, you are discharged from this ward"

part three

Conversation concluded. So, as I am writing this my future lies uncertain. This is my last ward entry before I am released a little later on today. Most people would be, indeed are, happy to be discharged. But, for me, I feel cheated in some way. As if they haven't done anymore than contain me. Maybe they were right. Perhaps I do crave attention and that is why I am self-harming so badly. Are they right? Time will tell. If I carry on as I have done within a home environment then he has been proved wrong. I don't know what will happen next. I just know that my time has ended and that it is time to move on.

Its five o'clock in the afternoon and my bags and my anger are packed away. God, I hope the real world is more ready for me than I am to it. Being released scares me, especially since no real issues have been addressed. Quiet and peace, those things promised by my GP have turned into something far greater the I ever expected. So, goodbye ward. I just hope that all you fore-saw remains true. Somehow I don't think this is over yet. Still, too much to do and examine. I guess I'll have to do it on my own

the crying shore

Free the soul - eat the flesh
Through a dedicated body I enhance my soul
Through external suffering my soul shall be free
Through listening to a deeper voice I will understand
Free the soul - eat the flesh

I am all that I can be
This moment - this time - I dedicate to you
My being is but through your calling

Without you I am nothing
Without you I am without hope

I think
I touch
I kiss
I depart
This is all I am
This is all I can be

There can be nothing more than this
Free the soul - eat the flesh

THE MASTER OF GAMES – V

Anticipation was at play early the next morning. Andrew wasn't sure if Claire would keep to the deal in the new light of day, but he hoped she would. If this barrier was crossed then, he knew, he could safely conclude the formation of a sexual relationship of some kind. Maybe once, maybe more: The game required more. He wanted to hold her soul within his hands. Her very presence had to be his. Breakfast was the time, he knew this, it was to be his moment or try at the very least. In retrospect, this moment would either enhance or destroy their relationship. They had both made sexual innuendoes to each other over the past weeks. Now? Now no more. He'd worked for this. Sure he was scared of rejection but, it had to be this moment.

He finally heard her footsteps upon the stairs and his heart started to pump faster. His mouth went dry. His erection grew. His palms started to sweat as the footsteps grew closer. He readjusted his bed position in order to accept his breakfast. He stroked his penis. A knock came upon the bedroom door. He reconsidered his bed posture and wiped his hands upon the bed sheet.

"Come in."

The door started to open. His heart pumped even faster. He ruffled his hair and then he waited. The door opened fully and there stood Claire, holding a breakfast tray for two, dressed in a dressing gown.

Deep down Andrew cried "shit."

"You backed down!" He said uninterested in her offerings.

"Are you joking?" She replied, placing the breakfast tray upon a table by the bed.

"About what?"

"About the topless bit."

"Were you joking ," he enquired, "when you made your deal?"

"Yeah, er, of course." Liar he thought.

"I don't think so. Anyhow, you've cheated now so what is the point?"

"I made you breakfast at least."

"I wasn't interested in the breakfast. That was more a, ah, how can I put this? A secondary consideration."

"I don't understand." Claire picked up one of the cups of tea and offered it to him. He shook his head so she began to drink out of it.

"Do I have to spell it out to you?"

"I don't understand?"

"Is there an echo in here?"

"I thought you wanted breakfast in bed."

"I did do. But I was more interested in, ah, in seeing your breasts to be frank about it." He hoped he wasn't blushing.

"Not much to see." Claire joked, "I hardly fill an 'A' cup."

"That doesn't bother me."

"They'll only disappoint you."

"I doubt it."

"My god! You actually are serious about this, aren't you?"

"Aren't you?"

"I, er, guess that, umh, that I thought of it as a joke."

"I've already explained this," Andrew said reaching for the other cup of tea.

"Why do want to see them?"

"Because I'd like to."

"What exactly are you saying here?"

"Oh, that's pretty simple really. What I'm saying is that I'd very much like to see you topless."

"Do you fancy me or something?"

"No or something. Yes I do. Why is that a problem?"

"Well apart from me and you, there's Donna and Mike to consider for starters. Yes, its a problem."

"So you don't return the desire. Fine. No, that's cool. Let's just forget this conversation happened."

He took a drink from his cup, staring at her in the eyes as he did so. His face could not lie. It conveyed to her his disappointment and, more importantly for him, his desire of wanting her. Claire fidgeted upon the bed, as if uneasy. There was a silence for a few brief moments before she finally spoke, sensing that Andrew would not be the one to break the atmosphere of discomfort that had enveloped the room.

"I'm not sure I want to," she said.

"Now it's my turn to ask what do you mean?"

"I, er, don't quite know. I have these feelings towards you but I'm not sure what they mean. I'm, sitting here dying to get into bed with you but yet, umh, and yet I don't want to."

"I think that's called guilt, isn't it?"

"Don't you feel the same?"

"Not really. My consideration was quite simple. Donna or you and that's all. If I can use the word, you 'won'. I find you far more attractive than Donna in every sense. I've given it a lot of thought and you win every time. But, hey," he replaced his cup of tea, "if you don't feel the same way then fine. I just end up looking stupid and responsible for destroying our close friendship. I must say though, I thought that you felt the same way."

Claire brought her legs up onto the bed and, facing him straight on, sat there cross-legged with her fingers toying with her cup.

"I think I do feel the same way. But, I can't simplify it in the same way as you. I love Mike for many different reasons. With you I feel, fuck, I don't know, I just want to sleep with you. I want you both for different reasons. I can't make the choice as easy as you at the moment."

"Hey! Hey! I'm not saying that we should have any kind of exclusive pairing or anything."

"What do you mean?"

"Well, as far as I am concerned, you can have us both. I don't have a problem with that. All I know is that we both seem to want the same thing but with different boundaries. You want us both and that's fine with me but, I have to honest, and say that I fancy you like mad."

"Okay. I understand that clearly enough. Ah, shit!" She ran her fingers through her hair and sighed. Andrew thought he saw tears forming within her eyes.

"If you're not sure about this then lets forget it," he replied. "I don't want this to get all heavy."

"If, if you could, er, do anything right now, what would it be?"

"Well, to be honest", he said, sensing some salvation, "I have this craving to reach across and undo the belt to your dressing gown and then to kiss you all over."

"This is getting weird. I really am stuck here. What if Mike finds out?"

"Why should he?"

"I don't know."

"Its your call Claire. I've told you how I feel, and now? Well that's up to you."

"You know, if I could do anything right now, without thought or consideration, I'd allow you to fed your craving." She placed her cup of tea upon the bedside table.

"Go with what you feel."

"You're just trying to get me into bed. You don't care how it happens."

"The penny has finally dropped."

Then there was silence. The conversation had reached its peak. Andrew looked at Claire and Claire looked downward. He thought he had blown it. Game over and he was the loser. But, within the silent period, with tension growing, Claire placed her hands onto her thighs before, slowly, moving them up to the belt. She's going to do it, Andrew thought, she is going to give herself to me. But there she stayed. A hand upon each end of the cord that contained her. He thought he saw the tears again in her eyes and then her heard her sigh. As she breathed outward, her hands pulled the cord and released the belt. For a brief second, or so, nothing happened but then she drew her hands away from her thigh area and placed them either side of her body. The dressing gown opened to reveal its treasure as Claire tilted her head backwards.

"God, I hope this is the right thing to do." She preyed to no one in particular. "God, I hope it is."

The she brought her head forward and gazed directly at Andrew.

"Are going to offer me a space within you bed, or not?" She asked meekly.

"Sorry." Andrew threw open the bed clothing on the other side of the bed and Claire slipped in, removing her dressing gown. For a moment it was a weird scene. Claire lay under the bed clothes, which she had pulled up to her neckline. She was lying on her back, eyes facing the ceiling. He lay next to her, on his side., propped up by one arm, looking at her naked before him, separated only by the fold of the bed clothes. The moment hung a bit longer, perhaps too long. It made the moment false, fragmented, removing the natural element of those first touches. Only words would progress this uneasiness and cut threw the strange feelings that they clearly both felt.

part three

Andrew said them first, in an attempt to restore what he had wanted to be a perfect moment.

"I've waited a long time for this moment." Shit! It was a cliché. He cursed himself for being too stupid and unimaginative. But it was too late.

"I'm nervous," she replied quietly.

"Do you still want to do this?"

"Don't make me think about it. Let's just take it as it comes. Help me forget the guilt and make the first move quickly."

He raised himself up, using his propped arm and bent over where she lay. Andrew thought he'd touched heaven as his mouth met hers. The embrace grew. Friendship kisses became kisses of passion. Tentative touches on each other's bodies became embraces and searches for pleasure. The morning melted away as if their hot bodies had melted it like ice.

The next morning, as it always is, was the tester. The reaction to the previous day may be taken either way. Too much pressure and regret or loving and happy. The hadn't left the bed all day, except to grab some wine. They'd fed themselves with each other in between joints and glasses of Chablis. Andrew awoke first. His body was curled around Claire's. She lay with her back to him, his arm draped over her side, his hand clasped between both of hers. His other hand lay trapped between her legs. He wanted to kiss her but was afraid of spoiling it all. He wanted a cigarette but knew that such action would cause too much movement. He thought about this dilemma for a few minutes and, in the end, snuggled deeper into her, pressing his face against her hair. He kissed her head. She stirred and Andrew panicked. He froze mid-kiss.

"I was dreaming of you," she said waking slightly. She turned around to face him and slipped her arms around him.

"I think I'm in love," she mumbled as she kissed him upon the lips and then lay down for more sleep.

Andrew's body relaxed and soon they were both at the place of dreams. Sometimes, Andrew thought as he fell asleep, life is good and luck smiles and that, at the current moment, he was king of the world.

THE BOOK OF HURT – Pt7

November 1999

Friday **5**

I'm home. Depressed Hooray! The people that had been 'helping out' whilst I was in hospital have seemingly been helping themselves to whatever they desired. My two cats looked in bad condition and the house looked even worse. It took me four hours to clean the mess left by these people and, I might sound ungrateful, but I'd expected, at the very least, a little respect towards my property, if not to myself.

Anyhow, that's all said and done. Now I feel pretty strange being within this home environment but I can't tell why. Its great to be home, don't get me wrong but I feel that parts of my house are alien to me. Perhaps this is because of my having other people around who have moved things, put them out of their place, but I don't think so. Even after tidying and replacing everything I still feel that way now. I am a stranger within my own world. The possessions that surround me do not cushion my social place but form barriers and promote 'no go' areas. I am afraid to touch or use anything. At this present time I am sitting upon the floor, cross-legged, in front of a dead fire writing these words whilst being aware of their unimportance. So, why do I keep writing? Well, to bring to the surface that which is, was, familiar to me. I no longer feel the same person having been on the ward. My brain and my body, although part of me, seem to behave in ways that are new to me. My hands, for instance, now shake and looking through my eyes is like sitting in an armchair in the back of my head. My balance is impaired, often causing me to fall or stumble. Its the drugs that cause these sensations, I know that, but their effects are enhanced by this alienation I feel within my own home. Maybe such alienation is also the result of the drugs but I can't be sure.

As I write with my right hand, my left hand is touching and stroking a statuette that had been given to me by someone very special. Consequently the figurine has also held that same importance. Yet, now my fingers no longer caress those familiar lines but fumble around the head, the body, without invoking any kind of recollection or comfort. My memory no longer draws up the images that it use to. No longer do I see images of Kate within its shape. No longer do I feel the happiness that it had brought me prior to my hospitalisation. I feel, in fact, the need to crush it. To smash it into tiny pieces. To render it insignificant and void. I resist from doing so only by holding on to the chance that its familiarity will return. I am a ship at sea with no mast. Just floating with the tide. I no longer have direction. I am just being.

Reflection and recollection become strange within such a world. Now that I have been 'processed' I find that I no longer fear the system but, rather, that I belong to it. The system has disjointed me, abstracted me from reality and caused me to view things through different eyes. Things that were once natural become alien and alien things become natural. Running a razor blade across my skin excites now rather than disgusts. The thought of death has become a reality rather than just an idea that was toyed with on occasions. In fact, suicide has a permanent place within my self.

Death is a funny thing. Most people, although they may not admit it, live in fear of it. The afterlife, heaven, call it what you will, scares people in to considering that our lives are more than just minutes, hours, days, years passing, that brings death closer. This fear holds them back. Risk is considered a necessity only when it has to be. They become scared of chance and lean more towards the familiar. Yet, I do not have this fear anymore. Realising that nothing lies beyond life itself has released me from the cage that protects from risk and chance. I feel that everything I do that involves the chance of death becomes lighter in magnitude for I know that there is nothing else out there and if I die then so be it.

We all need to peel away at this cage of protection. We need to break ourselves free, to embrace our fears and to act as we wish. Somebody once said 'that the only difference between sane and insane people is that sane people think before doing whilst insane people just do'.

I rather like this saying. There is an element of truth to it. I, personally, rather favour the insane side. It contains no barriers and holds little concern for social functioning. I know we are all social actors but why should this stop us from just being.

On my first day out of hospital I went in to an electrical shop to enquire about some mobile phone equipment. Whilst discussing this with one of the staff a man entered with a delivery. The staff member, who had been talking to me, had to deal with the delivery. Left on my own for a few minutes, I remembered that I had a tape, which I had just bought, sitting in one of my pockets. So, I took the tape out and placed it within one of the store demonstration music centres. I love the first track played and, subsequently, turned up the volume and began to dance to it. After the track had finished I removed the tape from the machine and placed it back into my pocket. To my amazement the delivery man and the staff member were both looking at me in a strange way. When I enquired if anything was the matter they had both looked sheepish and muttered 'no. no,. everything is fine'. The delivery man left and I continued to talk about phone accessories. However, the staff member seemed more on edge since the dancing display and so I left the shop. I had thought that I was at fault. But was I? I merely acted out my desire whilst he was bounded by social rules. I concluded then, as I do now, that the problem was his, not mine, for it was his barriers that were affected rather than mine, for I challenged him, not the other way around. In doing so I had taken him to a place he had been unlikely to have experienced before. I was just doing and it was he who was reacting. Now I realise the power that this freedom I displayed held over the scenario. He had to react to me and not I to him. I was the one in control and it felt good. Maybe my philosophy to 'free the soul' will turn out to be a good one.

At this present time my inner thoughts are chanting this 'free the soul, eat the flesh', as if a monk. It may seem strange but it can only be the answer. It is not enough to stop doing merely because a few people find it strange. If you can rationalise it then do it. Why give a shit about someone else's problem. Free the soul. Let it lift you beyond the social boundaries and place yourself within your own needs, wants and desires. Sure, others may not understand you, but that is their problem. Insanity can only be termed when in comparison with others. A woman dancing in her room can not be judged. The same woman dancing when within a supermarket can. Why is this? They are the same actions. The answer, of course, is that socially supermarkets and their users expect others to act in a certain way. Go beyond these boundaries and they label you as mad. Its a crazy world.

Maybe I am still a little bit mad but I find the 'free the soul' ideology to be an encapsulating one. I find that it is a multi-faceted statement for it can be used in many ways at the same time but its one philosophy within a world of many but it is one that, despite growing within a psychiatric ward, works well for me. As I write this I feel calmness, an inner peace that says 'I am not afraid' and this brings joy to my heart.

THE MASTER OF GAMES – VI

They made love twice that next morning before Andrew got up to make the breakfast. Half an hour later, upon his return, he re-entered the room that contained a sleeping Claire, carrying a tray which he placed beside the bed. He sat upon the mattress and, reaching across, pushed away the hair that had fallen across her face. She stirred and Andrew felt scared. Not of her waking but of the fire that was beginning to ignite within his heart. This was a game after all. 'Easy in - easy out' that was his motto. Yet, he wasn't feeling how he should have been. He felt desire, passion, that was something much, much more than just a conquest. The game was, seemingly, turning into a resemblance of love.

His second stroke awoke her.

"Hi, sleepy-head. I was beginning to wonder if you were still alive."

"Me to," she said, throat dry and creaky. "Is this all really happening?"

"Don't think about it."

"How can I not. I'm sleeping with my boyfriend's best friend. Worse is the fact that I am actually enjoying it.

What time is it?"

"Half past ten. Why?"

"Because today we are off to Wales for a few days. I've rented a cottage for a while."

"Are you serious?"

"But of course I am. I thought that it would be good to go away somewhere where no one knows us and where we can just be natural."

"Okay, but..."

Something was happening here again that Andrew didn't like. This was only the second day of their 'relationship'. He knew for a fact that she had not left the bedroom since, apart from doing the necessary toilet things. Yet, somehow, she had managed to book a cottage for a few days. The conclusion was obvious. she had booked the cottage before the affair had started. How else could she have done it? Who's game was this? Andrew had thought it was his, but it was rapidly becoming clear that he was not the one in control. Did he care? The game was, after all, turning into something more for him. Of course he cared. He wasn't at the controls. Being unable to control was a new experience for him. Worse was the fact that Claire had obviously began a process of game playing herself. He decided that the only way to tackle this was head on.

"When did you made all these arrangements?"

"The day before you came to stay. Why? Is anything the matter?"

"I'm not sure. How did you know that we'd be together? I mean, oh, you know what I'm saying."

"I didn't. I just thought that it would be a fun place to be. It is summer after all and what better to spend the week than away from this place."

Andrew was mot truly convinced. He redressed his question. "How did you know that I'd come with you?"

"I didn't know, I just guessed that you would be up for it. You do want to go, don't you?"

"Now. after what has happened, yes. But, if we hadn't ended up in bed together than I'm not so sure. I mean, how could I spend some time in a small country cottage wanting you as badly as I do? I'm more freaked out about the fact that you pre-arranged this. Its almost like you know something was going to happen between us. That you knew we would end up in bed together. I'm not complaining, don't get me wrong, but I'm curious as to your intentions prior to us making love."

"Okay. What do you want me to admit to you? That I've fancied you for a while? That I seemingly want you as much as you want me? Is that what you want to know?"

"Fuck it. Its not important anyhow. Spending a few days away with you would be great. Forget the details, let's just go and have some fun before Mike gets back."

He still was unconvinced by her answer. He was pretty certain that there was something else going on here that he just couldn't picture. Something not right. However. he went with the flow of it all whilst his brain rushed into over-drive as he fought to retake control.

Soon, they were packed and off to Wales. The journey was pretty uneventful, apart from the fact that Andrew was given a blow-job whilst driving at 90 miles an hour. It took them five hours to reach the cottage that Claire had rented. It was rested upon a hill, overlooking a wooded valley. He had to admit that it was nice. As soon as he had stepped out of the car he had felt relaxed and contented. This was made all the better by Claire coming up from behind and sliding her arms around his waist.

"Nice place," Andrew said, "a couple of days here should be pretty good. I'm knackered, I'd love a joint."

"Umh, that sounds wonderful," Claire purred.

part three

They entered into the cottage and explored. It was a typical Welsh farmhouse cottage with two rooms downstairs and two up. They playfully thought over who was to sleep where and whether they should sleep together but it was just fun. They both knew that they would sleep together and sleep where ever they fell. They could hardly keep their hands to themselves as they off-loaded the car and began to place their few possessions around the place. They had brought their own tape player, which was fortunate as the place had no music playing facilities. Andrew inserted a Van Morrison tape, and sorted out a fire, whilst Claire cooked. She cooked pasta, which was served with a bottle of Chardonnay, and they ate upon the floor in front off a roaring flame.

"Feeling better now?" Claire asked.

"Yeah, its a nice place. The company is a little stuffy but, apart from that, yeah, its great."

"You cheeky bastard!" She picked up a cushion and threw it at him. Andrew retaliated, grabbing another cushion from the sofa and hitting her around the head with it.

"Oi! Right that's it! Gloves off. Prepare for a pillow fight!" She was laughing as she reached forward, pillow in hand, and swiped Andrew upon the shoulder. They returned each other's blows until, tired from play fighting, Claire fell into Andrew's arms. They kissed. Nothing more, just kissed.

"I'm falling for you," she announced as she broke away slightly.

"And I for you."

"Is this really going to work? Certain people will hate us when they find out," said Claire.

"Certain people will just have to get use to it. Anyhow, who gives a shit about other people. Are they going to find out anyhow?"

"What do you mean 'are they'?"

"Well, who knows what will happen once this trip is over? You may go back to Mike, or I to Donna. We might just carry on behind people's backs, without anyone knowing."

"Carey knows," Claire interrupted. "I had to leave her a message, seeing as she didn't come home last night either. I hope that she's okay." Claire said a little concerned. "She's been gone two nights." She giggled slightly. "She did say it was probably gonna be a hot date."

"Well, she's unlikely to tell anyone."

"No, but she will have opinions."

"And what is her opinion likely to be?"

" Most probably that we should be honest about all this. Tell no lies. That cheating is wrong and that we should come clean."

"And what do you say?"

" I say that I'm not too sure. I want to be with you but I also feel sorry for Mike. He doesn't deserve this, neither does Donna. Perhaps honesty is the only way. Would our relationship still be the same, if it were out in the open?"

"You mean, is this only working because of how we're doing it?"

"Yeah, I guess."

"I can't answer that. All I can say is that I wanted to sleep with you and, now that I have, I would like something deeper that just sex. Does that answer your question?"

"I feel the same way." She licked at the cigarette papers that contained hash and tobacco. "Sod it! Lets go public upon our return."

"Okay. That's not a problem." He held a lighter to ignite her joint. "I can't believe that this is happening. I thought about this occurring within my dreams but never thought it would happen."

Claire exhaled. "Strange how life ends up, isn't it? A few weeks ago I would never have done this. Now? Now I wonder why I waited so long."

"I think that we should agree, right here and now, that despite how we feel, we never mention the word 'love'. I hate that word. As soon as it is said everything falls apart or cracks appear in the relationship. Are we agreed?"

"Umh," she exhaled again, "I can't agree more. No love just a relationship. Love ties you down and destroys your soul. I love you," she started laughing.

"Give me some of that joint or I'll love you back!" She passed it over.

"Don't want that now. Do we?"

They spent the rest of the night enjoying each other mentally and physically. As Claire slept, Andrew thought. It was out of control, as far as the game went. Is this really what he wanted? His heart was urging 'yes' but his head was telling him to slow down a little and take stock. He hadn't planned on loosing Donna when the game was started, let alone loosing Mike and a few others as well. Their little 'dinner circle' would be ruined but what the fuck. It was cliched anyway and needed some thing or someone to give it a shove. But, where was all this going and who was directing? Claire had said that Carey knew.

part three

So, already things had progressed past the line that he had drawn upon the game. He wanted to run with it, allow it freedom, but his gut instinct told him that it was more hassle than it was worth. Yet, in a sense, he knew he was powerless now to Claire's desires and needs. He had fallen for her badly and, seemingly, her to him. Maybe they had a future together, maybe not, but they had something going that was good for them both it seemed. His last thoughts, as he drifted off to sleep next to her, were that, in the end, he just wanted to be with her for now. Tomorrow? Well, that could wait until then. Within the back of his mind he heard himself talking the unmentionable word, 'love', and it scared him.

FLESH OF DREAMS (6)

    When Tiko called again my head was buzzing with a million questions. She positioned herself upon one of the sofas, as per normal, and I chose the other. We sat facing each other for a few minutes before she spoke.

"I thought you might have had questions for me?"

"I do. I'm just trying to see where I lie within this world and the real."

"But this is real. Can't you see? You have legs, arms, a body, everything. You can even taste what you eat. You can think clearly here, be yourself or anyone else. I thought that was what you wanted. You certainly, well in my experience, wanted, as they all do, to enter into the Shore. To find a place within the globe."

"These globes scare me. I don't want an artificial world. I just want out of the darkness that is outside."

"You came to us, not the other way around. You should be happy here, creating your future."

"But is it real?"

"In what sense?"

"Is it me within the globe or someone who looks and talks like me, may even believe, that their globe is reality and that all they are after is my soul?"

"No. It is you within the globe. True, the person who entered will have a dual reality for a while, we call it "jet lag", and so these two fragments of yourself will make a whole. So, in a sense, you will be as alive as you are now. Not quite truth but reality none the less."

"And there is no other way to escape?"

"Within reality you have no substance. No body. Here, as I say, you can have substance."

"But what is this blackness?"

"It is you without form."

"But what does it mean? Where in reality do I exist? Am I a lost soul or what?"

"You certainly do have a lot of questions! I think the best way of explaining this is to start back at the beginning. Don't you think?"

"I just want to know."

"You live, in the real world, without form because you reside within someone else's mind."

"Who is this person?"

"I cannot tell you that for I do not know who it is."

"But how do I bring myself to the fore. To become, at least, equal in sharing the shape?"

"That I can not answer. Neither you, nor I, can do that. Only the one whose body you occupy can do that. They must, it would seem, want to acknowledge and bring you in."

"So, as well as the globe, there is another way through this darkness?"

"Some, few I might add, have chosen not to enter their globes. What happens to them I do not know, for I reside here." She opened her arms wide. "I know nothing outside of this place."

"So, what are the globes?"

"They are a place to make yourself real. The odds are against you. Very few opt-out of the globe life. Maybe they still live in their own darkness, maybe they achieved success. Who knows?"

"But what are they? Who looks after them?"

They become stored away until your death then they are broken. As to who looks after them, that is the teacher's job. I will look after your globe…"

"You'll be my god?"

"In a way, yes I will. Why does that scare you? Do you not trust me? Have I lied or mistreated you in any way?"

"No, you haven't but that doesn't make it right. Given the choice I'd rather be real than some artificial self. The thought of you being 'god' scares me though. Its not that I mistrust you. I don't know, it scares me, that's all."

"And who do you think controls the real world? All planets are globes. Some small, some large, yet all of them have teachers that look after them. If you choose to try and enter reality all you are doing is placing your self within the hands of some other teacher. Why trust them and not me?"

"Because, because, shit, I don't know. This place and reality seem so different."

"But, that is merely because you are not yet within your globe. Once you are, it will be as big and as real as the place you call reality. Reality is just another globe!"

"Do all the people that come here come from the darkness?"

"Most, though not all."

"If I understand this correctly, and correct me if I am wrong, I can either enter this globe," I pick it up from the table, "or live in another globe that only appears bigger because I am within."

"Correct."

"I've heard names in my darkness. I've heard the names 'Andrew' and 'Melissa'. Do you know what these names mean? How do they interconnect?"

"As I have said before, I know nothing outside of this place. There are many names used here when in reality names are unimportant."

"But they must mean something! The name 'Melissa' brought images, thoughts and feelings with it. As if it were a name I recognised, associated with. I saw tiny droplets of light through my darkness and, more importantly, something spoke to me. Directly to me, as if it acknowledged my existence and, as if it knew me well."

"They were probably just names you thought you heard. You have been so desperate to become real that you probably imagined their existence."

"No. No, I don't think so. I felt myself becoming, er, connected, if that's the right word, with whatever lies beyond the blackness."

"Take my advice and ignore these things. Your place is here," she pointed to my globe, "your future lies within your hands, being created as we speak. This is your home. Not the blackness, not even the Shore Hotel, it is here within your globe. I want you to see that this is the only way for you to become real and release yourself from the darkness that you currently reside in."

"Will the blackness go away once I am inside the globe?"

"Umh, let me say this. At present you reside in darkness and you come here through dreams. Once your globe is complete and you have fully entered it, with the jet-lag over, then you will no longer live this dual existence. You will meet this blackness you and become one with it within the globe. You will cease to dream of the Shore and become part of something much bigger. It is only now that your life is beginning. Let it happen. It was intended to be this way. Allow it just to flow."

"But I feel that whilst awake, within the darkness, I must at least try to free myself. I can't exist without trying. Its what keeps me sane. The knowing that there is something beyond it that, if I try hard enough, I can reach out and touch. Just hearing those few words made me feel strange, excited and hopeful. These are things that I have not felt here. Even within my globe I did not experience this feeling. It felt unforced, unnatural somehow."

She seemed annoyed at my constant questioning of what lay beyond the blackness. As I spoke she shuffled and made deep throaty noises, as if she were disinterested. Her annoyance was, also, seeming to grow in magnitude.

"Do you want me to help or not? You called me to show you the way and yet you wish to move in the opposite direction. I don't understand why you bother. You can't have both, that is not possible. Choose your direction and stop wasting my time. You can go with your feelings or go with my experience. It is your choice but, make it now, for I don't wish to waste time if it leads to you trying to reach through to the darkness. You know what I feel, now make your choice."

"Its not that simple."

"It has to be. Your globe will soon be ready. So, it has to be."

"Who will live upon my globe? Is it just me, or will there be others?"

There will be others. Millions of people. You must make your choice now."

part three

My brain was in overdrive. Within the blackness I feel more alive than I do here. Especially since I have heard words. Yet, I may never escape the darkness and have to spend a lifetime of emptiness. If I choose the globe then I am going against my instincts but, in doing so, will be able to have an existence that will at least allow me to live a full life. Its hard to decide. I understand why she is called the 'Sanity Assassin' for I am truly on the verge of sanity at the moment.

"Make your choice."

I feel pressured. Unable to decide which way it should be.

"I can't," I complain.

"Make your choice," she repeated. I sensed that she thought she was loosing the battle and, maybe, she was. My instinct told me not to go into the globe. That is was made by hand rather than natural. Yet, on the other hand, the globe would become real to me eventually.

"I don't think I can enter the globe," I blurted, surprising even myself.

"So, I have wasted my time!" she exclaimed with clear anger.

"No. No you haven't. It just doesn't feel the right thing to do. I have many questions about that which lies beyond the blackness that I must try and answer. I know how you feel but I must go with my deepest feelings. I know you won't understand but I can't explain it any other way."

"I must say I am surprised. When you called me you wanted life now you seem content to live in your blackened world clutching at tiny fragments from time to time that seem so important but which, also, advance you no further forward."

"I know. I'm sorry."

"I think, in the long run, you will be. Later you will regret what you have said and done here today. However, in the end, it is your choice."

I looked at the globe that I still held. In the beginning it held so much and yet now it resembled a prison of glass. I placed it back upon the table.

"So, this is your final choice?" Tiko said as she leant forward and collected my globe.

"I just feel it has to be," I reply.

"Fine. You will not come back here again." She lifted my globe above her head and threw it violently to the floor. It smashed into a thousand pieces and everything stopped. I was thrust back within my black prison. The drone was

part three

still going on and on and I felt sad that I would no longer dream of the shore hotel and what it had to offer. Now, it was all or nothing. I had to break through to the other side. I wasn't quite sure how, I just knew that I had to do it.

DIRECTION

crossing through barriers
within an empty world
that holds me tight
turns me as it might
and makes me responsible for all those times
for all of its secrets and all of its crimes
leaving me lifeless
as fluid as dreams
I move so gracious
within her screams
and I don't really care
if there is nobody there
to capture the form
of yet another brilliant storm
that spins around inside of her head
I've opened the book and heard it read
and white and black
she lies through the back
dazily dancing to another track
whilst I sit here with deeper contemplation
opening blooded eyes to new information
that I shape and I mould till it flows away
and how many time have I heard it say
sometimes things get better this way
when we push them further and further apart
and keep them away from an empty heart
and my fingers are bare and down to the bone
there are things I should have known
through the entangled images I have been shown
with these experiences I should have grown

part four

"fluid within
tainted rainbows"

IMAGES OF BEING

empty hands - silent voice
cries with emptiness - isolation
incubation - vacuous spaces
turn around me - within me - for me
there is nothing - not now
but dreams - shattered and broken
I am dragging my thoughts - within murky water
and treading the waves - waves goodbye
to yesterday's child
who cries a false name - its a game
I - you - them - are playing
surrounded by conformity
scared to move - inward - and outward
with arms akimbo - I stand in limbo
breathless and bracing
I sing into the wind
a similar name - without speaking
as I move so gracious - with fear of loathing
and clothing my flesh
with items of uncertainty
I walk as naked - as a baby
hands held in prayer - is anybody there
to answer my wishes - punish with kisses
that offer me hope
and beckon me onwards
to you - and who - walks through
my dreams - and screams
in a voice- I can not remember
to a soul that has long since flown
with no direction
home

TO HELL WITH UNCERTAINTY [e]

'Umh, not bad', he thought, 'not bad at all'. He was standing within his scared space. Viewing himself through the mirrors that held many secrets. The mirrors that beckoned him, demanded him and controlled him. They called for him to offer himself to them in new ways. Ways that were normally considered sexually deviant and perverse. He, in turn, gave in to them. Refusing to accept that it was the real self that he gave. To him, he offered another part of his being, not the true him, but the him that was reflected back. The opposite to himself. A barrier that satisfied the mirrors' demands and satisfied his need for separation from the events that the mirrors witnessed. It was a trade-off that worked well.

This time he was witnessing his opposite self standing in front of the mirror whilst dressed in woman's clothing. He studied himself. Drawing up the hem of the skirt that he wore until the suspender belt and stocking tops revealed themselves. He ran his hands across the different silks, further stiffening his erection, and groaned. He had already switched himself off from the real world and was lost within thoughts of pleasure. A pleasure that also, paradoxically, contained hatred within it. As he watched his reflected self he began to expand upon this hatred, allowing it to grow and overcome the thoughts of satisfaction. As far as he was concerned, such hatred was not put upon himself directly but upon the reflection that stood before him.

"Look at you! Who the fuck is going to like you?" He spoke out loud. "You're sick, vile, fucking disgusting. I hate you so fucking much. A fucking drag queen, that's what you are. A filthy drag queen that no one cares about"

He let the hem of the skirt drop back down again. He ran his hands across the skirt's material, rubbing at his erection lying underneath. With his free right hand he fumbled his way to the back of the skirt and began to undo the zip. He slid his hand into the opening and began to feel his arse through the underwear. As he did so, he occasionally pulled the underwear material together and upwards causing it to cut into his testicles and anus inducing pain. He played with himself in this way for a few minutes before allowing the material to slip from his grasp. His right hand slipped itself inside of the underwear, its silky smoothness caressing the back of his hand. Stroking each buttock in turn with this hand his other grasped at the erection and, through the skirt material, began to masturbate.

As he did he knelt down upon his knees and bent forward slightly. The front reflection showed him still grasping at the material and the erection whilst the back mirror displayed the movements of his right hand which he eventually slipped out of the zipper opening. He bundled the skirt up at the back to reveal his underwear. Again he stroked his buttocks but this time through the material of his panties. He was becoming turned on. His desire, to caress and touch, was being over ridden by another urge that was welling up inside of him. He wanted to cause pain upon his body. The right hand pulled the knicker material to one side and he dug his fingernails into his buttocks and scratched himself. He did it again, deeper this time, causing deep red lines to appear across his arse. It was painful but not enough to satisfy his growing urge. He slid his hand downwards, towards his anus and, once located, he began to gently rub it. The gentleness did not last long. He extended his forefinger and began to force it into his anus. He pushed it in up to the knuckle and the began to ram it in and out. It wasn't painful, not yet anyhow, but it made his urge grow. He had a vibrator beside him. He used it anyway. Forcing it up and deep inside. He turned it on and the mechanics of the vibrator began to work their magic deep inside. It wasn't enough.

He hated stopping mid-way through his masturbations as it broke the contact between himself and the mirror. It made him become himself again but this time he felt he had to. Removing the vibrator, he went in search of something with a bigger circumference to it. He went into the bathroom and searched around within the cabinets and window shelf. He found a shampoo container upon the bath surround. It was thick and round. He also grabbed some baby oil, to lubricate his arse, before heading back into the bedroom and the awaiting mirrors. He positioned the bottle mid-way between the mirrors. He rubbed again at his now semi-erection whilst he focused his attention back to the mirrors. It took a few minutes to reach the point that he had left, rubbing at his penis and his anus and cursing himself further but he was now ready to complete this particular masturbation.

He stood between both mirrors and lifted his skirt. He held it, bunched up, within his left hand. Opening up the baby oil bottle he squirted some of the liquid over the vibrator and began to smear it over the top and sides. He discarded the baby oil and repositioned himself over the vibratin plastic. His right hand held it steady as he lowered himself down upon it. Using the vibrator to push his underwear to one side he rubbed his anus against the tool before he began to insert into himself. He felt the top funnel of the vibrator enter him. Viewing through both mirrors he watched as he lowered himself deeper and deeper onto it. By the time it reached the vibrator's maximum circumference he was already wondering if his body could accommodate it all. The strain was painful but it was a different sort of pain. There was a pleasure within it. A sensation of pushing to the limit. He had done this before, with numerous bottles and things, but this was without doubt the biggest thing yet to be inserted within himself. He pushed down a little more, groaning as he did so. Once when he had done a similar act he had caused his anus to bleed as it stretched itself. He had found the blood a turn on, but it had only happened that once, despite his attempts to achieve such a status again. He felt like he was going to burst as he lowered himself even further down. His left hand let the skirt go and, sliding into the material began to masturbate and stroke his penis through the silk underwear. As he did so he began to move up and down upon the inserted plastic. Pushing it further upwards with every downward stroke made. He wanted to cum but he knew that he could stave it off for a little while longer. He had a grand finale planned. It was always that way. Sometimes he disappointed himself by cuming too soon but this time he as adamant, perhaps desperate would be a better word, that it would not happen to him today.

The vibrating tool was finally inserted to its maximum position. He looked into the forward mirror and saw the back reflection which was his arse filled with the thing. He began to remove his underwear. Stepping out of them whilst still in a crouched position. He re-examined the images reflected. He felt good. The images were pleasing. He bent a little further forward and, using his left hand, began to slide the vibrator in and out. His right hand slipped up his skirt and grasped the erection, flesh upon flesh, for the first time. He wasn't fully erect at this point, which was perfect as far as the plan went. An erect penis only meant that the session was almost at an end. A slightly limp penis gave him more time to enjoy the agony of having something so big inserted deep within him. More than that, it would allow himself to do other things before reaching his climax.

He pushed the stiff vibrator in and out until he grew bored with its offerings and he allowed it slip out completely. He ran his fingers around his anus. It felt slightly sore and expanded but it hadn't bled. As he did this he began to undo the blouse he was wearing. He started from the bottom, undoing each button as if cautious but excited. Once they were all undone he pulled open the blouse to reveal a silk chemise and placed the bottle back upon the floor. He slid the blouse off, followed by the skirt. And there he knelt. Dressed now only in the underwear. Within the reflection he could see his bulging penis which was standing fully upright. He placed a hand upon it and caressed it gently. He didn't want it to be fully erect, not yet anyhow, and the soft strokes administered finally allowed the intensity of his erection to dissipate. It soon reached the limpness required. He lay upon his back, with his legs wide open and took hold of his penis, which was pulled down between his legs. The head was rubbed against his buttocks and anus. As he did this he slid a finger inside of himself. He stretched the hole as far as he could and, once satisfied, removed his fingers and began to insert his own penis into his arse. He felt it enter, held in place by his hands, and began to fuck himself.

Within the mirror, the image was one that brought great arousal. He tried to keep his penis soft but the image displayed before him would not allow this to happen. As his erection stiffened it began to retreat from his arse. Soon it was standing proud again. He rubbed the head with his fingers and a sensation of arousal washed over him. It was unwelcome at the present. So much so that he stopped giving his erection the satisfaction it required and began, instead, to stroke other body parts. It took a few minutes before it began to wane. Once it had, he allowed it to go limp even more. He felt his bladder begin to call out to him. This was the point, the moment, that he was really after. He took hold of his penis between his thumb and forefinger and pointed it at himself. The bladder calling grew louder within his head as he tried to hold it back a little longer but the moment could not be sustained any longer, he had to let it go. Whilst directing his penis upward, he began to release his bladder. He used his muscles to force out the urine. The first wave reached his face and mouth, as did the second pulse. He licked at his lips and the allowed the dam to fully open. Urine gushed from his penis, splattering over every part of his body. He began to masturbate whilst doing so, sending splashes everywhere as he pumped frantically. With his free hand he began to smear the urine over the remainder of his body. His chemise became soaked with it. Occasionally he would bring his fingers up to his mouth to suck them clean before continuing with the spreading.

When he finally stopped pissing his whole body was covered. At this point his erection had returned. He thought about shitting himself but he wasn't really in the mood for it. He had done it before but today he had no real urge to go to that level. He continued to masturbate instead, occasionally licking at his fingers. The need to climax began to rise within him again. This time, however, he felt no need to hold it back. The reflections within the mirrors signalled that he had done enough to allow the satisfaction of orgasm. So, he concentrated upon that. Sliding his hand up and down the length of his penis. He thought about drinking the semen but declined the thought. He just wanted to ejaculate.

He looked at himself as he did so. Inside his head he was calling himself every degrading word he could think of. It turned him on, even if they did hold an element of truth within them. He was sure that not many masturbated as he did but, he concluded, that was not to say that it was wrong to do so as he did. Then it happened. It occurred quickly, catching him by surprise, as the first spurts exited his penis and planted themselves upon his chest. He stopped masturbating and watched, relaxed, as further bursts of semen deposited themselves upon his body. His hands began to smear it. He stroked it into his chest and around his thighs and continued to do so until the last drop of semen had been released.

Once it was over he closed his eyes and then rolled over to one side, away from the reflections. He felt his true self returning. He hated his reflection at times like these. All he wanted to do was remove the under clothes, shower down his body and wash his mouth clean of the excrement, urine and semen that he had welcomed before. He removed the garments and then sat naked upon the floor. He looked himself up and down and wondered if such acts would ever leave him. Whether or not he was destined to masturbate like this forever. Is this what 'normal' people do or was he unique in his quest to find total humiliation?

He cried after a while. He knew he took himself to new extremes. Levels that most people would not even entertain mentally let alone physically. He felt deviant yet, he also felt that his actions were out of his control. That they were driven by his desire. All this did not however stop the tears. He was lonely. Afraid to talk to others about how he felt and what he did. Such loneliness merely enforced his sense of isolation. This, in turn, only made him hate himself even more. It was a ride that he thought he could never climb off. That it was destined to always be this way. Yet, there was a key that would free him from such a lifestyle. It was just finding it. As it happened he didn't have to look very far. It found him eventually. He had always felt the seed of his salvation, deep within, but had never allowed it to flourish. Still, in the end, what did it matter who found who? The fact was he would eventually grow this seed and put an end to all this. It would just take time, that was all.

THE MASTER OF GAMES – VII

The first hour, driving back from Wales, had been silent. Both Claire and Andrew were seemingly quite in contemplation of what lay ahead. Mike would be back at the house by the time they got there, awaiting Claire's return. He would not be expecting Andrew to be in toe. Claire had told him a lie, had told him that she was going to spend a few days with a friend in Cambridge. Andrew had hoped to get there before Mike and then to depart whilst Claire and Mike talked. That had been the plan but Claire had changed it. She had said that she couldn't face Mike alone. Andrew was uneasy about being dragged into the end of their relationship but then, he already was involved. This was going to messy. A decade of friendships were about to be broken and shattered as if they had never mattered. Andrew had, over the weekend, given this careful consideration. Claire had appeared not to be so concerned. Her talk was of how she would tell Mike, not of what she might loose. It was a strengthening sign that Andrew took on board. She obviously wanted to be with him, no matter what the cost involved. This is madness, Andrew thought, as he drove. It was a game not a lifestyle change. It was suppose to happen once, twice maybe, then it was due to be put away and forgotten about. Yet, here he was only a few hours away from perhaps the biggest disruption his life had ever felt.

He glanced at Claire. "You okay?"

"Yeah, I guess so. I'm a little nervous but I'm okay." She reached out a hand and stroked his knee. "How about you? Think you can cope with it?"

"I'm not that sure actually. I, umh, I don't know.."

"Don't go cracking up on me now! We talked about this. We both agreed on how this was going to work. You would be there when I talked to Mike and I would be there, if you wanted it, when you spoke to Donna. That's what we agreed wasn't it?"

"Yeah, yeah, I know. But I'm not concerned about that. I'm concerned about the impact that it is going to have on all these people."

"You've changed your tune. I thought that you said it was all stale and in need of change anyway."

"I did."

"So what's new?"

"I feel uneasy about the way it all happened. I was just thinking that it might be a good idea if we finished with our respective partners before we announced that we were going to be together."

"No more lies you said. You said you couldn't face anymore secrets and lies. Is there something that you're not telling me?"

There was of course. He wanted to tell her that deep down all he wanted was a little bit of fun. He had never intended this. No, he didn't really want this. It was all a game, a challenge, that is what he did. But, he could never tell her this, not now anyhow.

He sighed. "I'm just concerned that's all," he said.

They withdrew, back into the silence. Andrew, once more, wondered where Claire had gone this morning. She'd offered no explanation and he hadn't asked. Maybe he should do so. Was this an element of mistrust? Perhaps she would offer the information if he asked. It wasn't as if she been cagey about it in anyway. He was obviously just feeling paranoid. Although her mood had changed when she returned, as if something had happened that cheered her up. Andrew was curious to know why. He needed to find a way to approach the subject. To ask her outright was to encourage confrontation. He didn't want that.

"Did you put any petrol in the car this morning?" he asked.

"No. I was going to but the garage was closed. Why, are we nearly out?"

part four

"Ah, yeah. Pretty much. Where were you this morning anyhow? I missed not waking up to you. I thought you had done a runner." He laughed nervously.

"I had to make a telephone call before we left. Why?"

"I just missed you that's all."

"I'm sure that you're big enough to cope on your own for a few minutes."

"You were gone a hour."

"Is there something wrong?" Claire said. "You make it sound as if I were up to something. I was only calling Carey to let her know what time we would be returning."

"Oh! Okay." More silence followed. Andrew chewed upon the information. She was lying, he knew that in an instant. For one, she had made the call between nine and ten o'clock. Carey wouldn't have been there, she would be at work by this time. She could have telephoned her at work but he doubted whether she would be able to talk for an hour. He felt nervous. He wondered what she was hiding. Maybe it was just none of his business. But it was his business. Already she was deceiving him. Denying him access. This was not a very encouraging sign. His feelings were becoming mixed and confused. On the one hand he had definite feelings towards Claire. That he wanted to be with her. On the other, he was aware of the game and its original intention. Moreover, there was the fact that he was no longer in control of what was happening. Perhaps this is what freaked him the most. He had never before allowed a simple matter of love to cloud his judgement. Before he had always been on the ball, so to speak, to be in charge of the events that surrounded him. Now he had dropped this control and, even worse, allowed it to pass to another. There was no way of regaining it now, he concluded, the time had passed him by. Within a few hours all hell would break loose and the game would take a new twist to it. It would run out of control and fill people with pain and hurt. He had never in his game playing life actually hurt anybody, that wasn't his style. His games had never been that vicious. But then times had changed. He was powerless within this. He could just tell Claire that he didn't want to continue this affair, and put an end to it all, but it wasn't that easy. Whilst in Wales Claire had categorically said that no matter what happened between them both Mike had to know what was occurring. It had to come into the open. It was the honest thing to do. Claire had, whether intentionally or not, forced Andrew into a corner. If Claire opened this can of worms then Mike, Peter and Donna would find out and he would loose them all, Claire included. So he had stayed silent. This was her game now not his and he bowed to her with an element of fear.

part four

They were now just an hour away from home. Conversation had been sporadic, to say the least, and tainted by both parties with an element of fear and anxiety.

"How are you going to tell Mike?" Andrew asked.

"I was just thinking about that. I've never told a boyfriend that I've been having an affair before. He's going to hate me. I don't want that but what can I do? I've got to be honest about this. I think I'll take him to the pub or something. Away from the house anyhow. You will still be there won't you? By my side I mean."

"Do really think that its such a good idea? Surely you'd be more a ease telling him without me being there."

"Are you chickening out?" She laughed.

"I'm as scared as hell." He said.

"Just because I appear cold about this doesn't mean that I'm not scared also. I've got a lot to loose over this. My whole world is about to change after years of being together. He's gonna hate me for the rest of his life. How can I justify to him what's been happening?"

"Do you have to?"

"I feel that I owe him that much at least."

"Yeah, I feel the same way about Donna. I'd like to tell her what's been happening as soon as possible. I don't want her to find out from someone else. That's why I think it would be better if I told her whilst you were telling Mike. I'm not trying to cop out or anything, its just that once Mike knows its going to spread like wild fire around the town. Are you sure that you really want me there?"

"Look, if you don't want to be there then that's fine. I want you there but its your choice. I'd be disappointed if you weren't but, as I say, its up to you isn't it?"

"Maybe we should tell them both together, at the same time."

"I don't think so."

"No. Neither do I really. I'm just trying to suggest options."

"Let's just do it as we said."

They exited the motorway. Now they were only about half an hour away from the inevitable. His heart was pumping. Conversation was dead. Even the stereo had been turned off. It was like waiting to die. He had never felt this sensation before. It consumed him but offered no comfort. Even the prospect of when it was all over offered no release from how he felt. It grew in intensity as they drove closer. He was aware that he had even

part four

slowed the vehicle down to lengthen their arrival. But time is linear and he knew that they would approach their destination sooner or later. Stretching it out only meant more agonising minutes and the growth of an even greater fear of what lay ahead.

Finally Claire said, "We're here. Shit." They drove into the town which, today, held an unfamiliarity to it. Everything seemed grey and washed out.

"I guess its time to face the crap," Andrew sighed, "I hope this works."

"You and me both."

The car entered the driveway of Carey's house and the two front doors slowly opened. Mike was at the house already, the doorway to the house was open. Andrew followed Claire into and through the house.

"Mike? Where are you?"

There came an answer.

"I'm out the back, in the garden. Can you grab a beer on your way through?"

"I think we could all do with one," Andrew said as he headed into the kitchen. Claire went to the back of the house. In the kitchen Andrew took his time. Hoping that it would all be over when he went outside. Hoping that Mike would not get up out of his seat and smack him one. Drawing out time he stood there for a few more moments before exiting armed with three bottles.

"Hi. Here you go." Andrew said as he handed a confused Mike a bottle and then gave one to Claire. They were both sitting at a table facing each other. Andrew declined one of the other seats and sat upon a wall, just slightly behind Claire.

"I passed my test!" Mike said triumphantly and rather nervously

"Cool," Andrew replied.

"How was Cambridge darling?"

"Ah, umh, I think we need to talk."

Mike looked at Claire and then at Andrew. Andrew could see Mike's confusion.

"About what?"

"About a few things that have happened whilst you were away."

part four

"Isn't that rather private?" Said Mike casting a glance towards Andrew sitting upon the wall.

"No. Its okay if he stays. In fact this includes all three of us."

"Okay." He was ill at ease but seemingly, from his manner and tone, did not expect the next sentence.

"So, what do you want to say?"

"I, I don't know really how to tell you. There is no easy way. I've been seeing someone else. I'm sorry to have to be blunt but its the best way."

"Need I guess who?" He shot Andrew a glance.

"No. I've been seeing Andrew since you left a week ago. It just sort of happened."

"I think we need to talk," Andrew said getting up and approaching the table. "Its all rather complicated."

THE BOOK OF HURT – Pt8

November 1999

Wednesday 16

I've been reading my diary from the 2nd October up until the 9th October with amazement. The philosophy that these pages hold still entices me to it's chest. 'Free the soul' has become my life. I like to view it as an art. Where everything that is done is done so with a purpose. Where, by releasing my soul, I can act and communicate as I desire. Its a paradoxical situation however for despite creating a well of honesty I have brought myself inward rather than out. As with so many things, the method and the actual doing are two very different things. Yes, I am honest about my life but I am also scared to death to walk through the streets. People make me anxious. I still sit with friends and wonder, with my time away and all that, if they now view me as different in some way. I may be freeing my soul but it seems that to do so is to do so at a cost. People just don't understand some of the actions I perform or become confused by my contradictions. Perhaps there is the possibility that I am not as sane as I think. Just because I view with a clarity does not make it the proper, social way to behave. Let's be honest about this. A person who decides to move away from social constraints, in an extreme manner, is bound to be judged by their social peers within a social context. More importantly, such people who move so freely are usually the ones that end up within psychiatric wards as their behaviour is considered to be anti-social in some way.

A few hours have now past since I wrote the above paragraph and I find my paradox coming back to haunt me. I am attempting to free my soul but, at the same time, I am eradicating my body through self harm. The actions that I perform upon myself are equally as much of a contradiction as the thoughts I have. My body is scared with my various self-harm methods and yet my body is my social passport. My actions upon my body destroy an easier social access. Will the cuts show in summer? Will I be forced to wear long sleeves in order for me to fit in or to deny my philosophy? Such questions worry me. They undermine my way of being. On the one hand I am free to act as I desire but yet I am aware, and concerned, as to my status and reading socially. Where does this leave me?

As I pick up the razor blade I am scared. I am scared of the harm it could inflict. Yet, I pick it up to inflict damage. I find that I twirl it around my fingers as I mentally pysch myself up to the pain it will cause. Then there is the first cut. A quick flick of the blade across the skin of the fore-arm. It stings a little, the blood gently bubbles to the surface. It does not run, just merges. I leaves me disappointed. The second cut made is deeper and longer. I feel its depth as it crosses my arm. Pain imposes itself upon me for a few seconds, never more, and is then replaced with pleasure. With the pleasure comes the blood swelling up within the wound until it overflows and runs down my arm. I just sit and watch it. Still scared but joyous. I gather a sense of desire to cut deeper still. Yet, there is a cautionary air about doing so. I do it anyway. I know my limit, what it takes to make me put away the blade, and that occurs between the third and fourth cut. So, I do it again to the point of crying out aloud. I replace the blade upon the bedside table and begin to inspect the wounds.

The last one lies deep. A trench has opened up across my forearm. It has great depth and is wide. Muscle and tendons become briefly visible before the blood begins to collect. It collects slowly at this level, for some reason, as if the cut had not been made. Slowly, however, it does begin to collect. It fills like a dam and then overflows to scary amounts pulsating. I watch it flowing down to my finger tips, running and collecting like a river until it drips with frequency off my fingers and onto the floor. This is my point. My maxim. I pry open the cut with my other hand, forcing more blood to collect and flow. Forcing the wound to open more and insert my fingers to touch those parts of my body that normally remain covered by the split flesh. It is the occasion that I live for. Just this moment. I don't do this in desperate times, I just do it when I feel its calling. Doing it during times of despair would cheapen it to merely a reaction. For me it is more of an action rather than the result of some other desire. It is, in itself, a complete process without such external influence or force. That is not to, as I have said, imply that it is purely enjoyable set of actions. Not only is there this conflict during but there is also the afterwards. The afterwards of social shame and hatred that I inflict upon myself for doing such things. I suppose, simply put, the act of self-harm is a love/hate relationship linked to private and public spheres where judgement is mine or theirs.

I don't know why I am explaining the act of cutting. Perhaps the hundreds of scares that reside upon my flesh need their story told. Maybe it clarifies, if only for myself, a self judgement, an explanation. All the cuts tell their own stories but each one has this pattern emerging through them. A fluidity that suggest a frequency. Each large cut is surrounded by smaller, more cowardly, slices. I had, perhaps still do, believe that these marks to be a part of my 'freeing the soul!' However, vanity and a sense of social placing have taught me that there are other ways to puncture the body and release that which lies inside. My use of the razor blades does not extend themselves to causing that unmentionable word - death. They merely mark me. I am too scared to touch my wrists with the narrow, sharpened metal. To inflict cuts that will kill me. I can only gather from this conclusion that blades are just not truly for me as a means of committing suicide. Pills seem to be that particular release. There seems, to me, to be more dignity about it. A classy way to go. Not the commonal, chemist collection but the harder stuff, the prescribed pills, that cause greater damage. Perhaps, it has just occurred to me, that the hospital may well be right in its conclusion of me coming in and out of accident and emergency on a regular basis. Its just a feeling I have.

I can't shake the desire that builds up inside of me. On the ward they put it down to games but if they are they are dangerous games to play. Especially upon myself. So far my quest has given me two unsuccessful hangings and several overdoses. The overdose I want to do again. No! These are not the right words to use. I don't want to do it again, I am compelled to do it. There is a force that I cannot control even though it comes from within me. Now, as I write, this force is growing. I want to touch death. To breath upon its face and allow my soul to walk away from my body. If only for that brief moment or ideally, for a lifetime. Needless to say I have the collection of pills neatly piled up in front of me. They are encased within an elliptical, bamboo box. I follow routine and run my fingers through them like they had come, rather delicately, from heaven. Small traces of blood begin to taint their purity.

I look at the still bleeding cuts and slices that cover my forearm. My 'good' arm reaches for a piece of toilet tissue, down beside my bed, and begin to soak up some of the red liquid. I don't want my pills tainted by my outside vileness. Today is a workday for my insides, and brain especially.

part four

Beside the bed also rests a particularly average Chardonnay wine, already uncorked, and I pour myself a glass after moping up as much of the blood as the tissue can hold. I raise the glass to my lips and drink the entire glass in one sitting. I pour a second glass but do not rush at it with the same vigour. As, apparently, the native Americans would say "Today it a good day to die." My eyes return to the pills. I run my hands through them again. I'm excited. This is real. I am scared. This is real. If I begin to ingest these pills I cannot turn back. Its weird but it doesn't happen that way for me. Once the mechanism is engaged it continues. out of my control, until the end. I pick 10 Diazepam from the box and study them. Half amazed that such innocent looking things can be detrimental to my health. The half pulsates warnings towards my ingestion of these pills. I know who is winning. The warnings are bleak. My life seems bleak at this point. Insignificant and fragmented from the real world. They fall upon deaf ears. I drink some more wine, refilling the glass. Sometimes, I guess life just deals a bad set of cards. There is nothing that can be done but to play the hand and bluff to its full potential and that is where I am at now. Bluffing myself through this life knowing that I have no real hand to play. I re-take the glass of wine from the bedside table. I take a mouthful of wine and swallow the 10 diazepam pills at the same time. Swirling them down with an ease and a comfort that normalises this situation. And so it goes on. The number of pills blurs into insignificance. I just keep on going. Wondering if I'll die or not. Scared feelings wash over me. I think about phoning a friend, to tell her what is going on, to seek some kind of response. I am not going to though. This is a one way trip with no return ticket.

Shit! Bugger! Fuck! The phone had rung and stupidly I had answered it. It was another old friend. It threw me. She guessed immediately that something was different. I continued to take the pills whilst talking to her.

She said, "Are you okay?"

"Fine. Yeah. Feeling good. How are you?"

"Are you sure?"

"Yeah, yeah. Why do you ask?"

"Your voice is slurred. I can hardly make sense out of what you are saying."

"I've just had a little to drink and a long day. No need to worry."

"I'm not convinced. You sound bloody awful."

"I feel it. But its cool."

"If you say so."

"I do. Trust me," shit I lied. "Tomorrow everything will be okay."

"I'm not happy."

"I'm sorry to hear that."

"No, I mean with you. Are you sure that you are okay?"

"Listen Donna, I'm fine. I'm painting the house tomorrow, that's why. Gonna plaint flags upon the roof and listen to the...."

"You're loosing me."

"I'm loosing myself. I was, what was I saying?"

"Painting roof tops?"

"No I wasn't! Was talking about ducking under the bar and showing that..."

"Mel? Mel? What's going on?"

"Nothing. Nuthing. Nutthing."

"You're lying." concern was evident.

"I just need to get out of bed, to be sick and get a glass of water."

"I'm gonna call an ambulance."

"Donna, I don't want....God! I'm going to be sick!"

"I'm calling the ambulance."

"Ah, Umh, are you sure."

"Yes."

"I just wanted to help myself. Hurt myself. I think I'm blacking out. I can't...."

FLESH OF DREAMS (7)

Blackness, droning, sounds like ice breaking cut through me. Without the Shore and the Sanity Assassin I feel lost. Tossing and turning with the turbulent waters of the blackness. I still have urges, desires, to be back there, to be whole again. More importantly, to exist within a world of communication. A place where I was heard. No, more that , where I was heard and listened to. An equality. But I chose my options. I gave away the globe life for one that, despite its uncertainty, feels right. I belong here. It, as I, are one. Parts of the same.

The Sanity Assassin stated that my isolation is due to my residing within the back of someone's mind. This news twangs strings for me. I had never before thought of such an occurrence and yet it appears, now, to make perfect sense. I now have the first building block from which to make my escape. I've even drawn fairly weighty theories as to what is happening and what can. The two names are apart of me. Of this there can be no doubt. One of them fits me but I cannot tell which one it is. I like them both. Yet, when I repeat their words I no longer see the pictures and memories for any of the two names. It frustrates me.

A lengthy period of time has passed since my last meeting at the Shore and my subsequent discharge. For one the realisation that I reside within means that I must push myself outwardly. That I must push past these barriers and project myself onto the outside. The question is how? Screaming for attention merely brought me a name and an action; to quieten down. I need much more than this. I needed to have total access to this body and other mind that entrap me. Perhaps, instead of working, or a least trying to work, from the inside out I should try to work on the inside from the inside. To manipulate those parts that are denied me. To show my acknowledgement. I get the feeling that these places already know of my existence but that, for some reason, they refuse to allow me access. I can hear, kind of, so that's on sense taken care off in its way. I've found that by careful concentration upon the drone I can hear other words. Words that I don't understand in their entirety but it is more than I had expected when I first dropped the globe. I'm not sure how to do this. Do I divide the brain into eye parts, voice parts, leg and arm parts and hearing parts? Work on each of them in turn? That sounds stupid but I'm retaining it as an idea. I can not give up on this. It remains my only hope now.

I concentrate further on this. How to break through? It fills and flows into what, seems to me, to be weeks. The levels grow deeper. Deeper than before. More inter linked with each other. Then it comes to me. A flash of inspiration, a knowable logic, call it what you will, but it came to me. Softly I speak to myself. Encourage a belief that I exist, that I am equal to the 'other' that restricts my right to bodily access. I am equal. I repeat this message again, then

part four

again and then again. Just as in my battle for the words 'Andrew' and 'Melissa' I continue my repetition but I must do so with a mammoth belief. I am equal. If I loose the belief I may never escape from this darkness that holds me. I am equal. No one is better, we are the same. I am equal. As the thought spins and spirals I continue with a deepened acceptance. Acknowledge me you bastard. We are one and the same. Wake up to me and allow me to grow and spread my stunted tentacles through your veins. No longer will I be caged. Labelled as something deep. Deep? Hidden? Am I a deformity? Does it matter? I must be released. I must expand into all the corners. To feel myself within all the entrails, within the blood and the bones. The very things that are on the outside. I must shake that which is my vessel.

The words flow through my sub-conscious. I reach the point where I no longer have to say them, they repeat themselves. Why doesn't the drone acknowledge me? Why am I still dancing this dance in limbo? Surely, by now, there must be a realisation that I am here. That my time has come to push forth. I am angry about this. My time spent within this nightmare has, if the Sanity Assassin was right, been no more than an imprisonment created by another part of me. Me! I trapped myself. I put me here. We are one and the same. My weakness is what left me within the dark. Abstracted and isolated from the remaining elements. Again, I ask, was I that bad? Did I need to be imprisoned? Does this matter now? Now that I have decided to become free. Part of me. I find the notion of self imprisonment slightly amusing. I'm sure I'd split my sides were it not for the anger. The fucking anger of wasted years. I am here. let me be born! Passivity is in my past, I want equality. To share, not to dominate. I want to find out what sort of person I am really. To show my hand and then decide.

I continue to push for this. As I do so my heart flutters with memories. It comes slowly at first as if being teased out from a very foreboding place. I remember being five, eight, ten, fourteen and I remember nothing. Images! Images of myself, a gendered self, a female self. I have a gender at last. Somewhere to place myself. A canvas to paint upon at long last. But why stop at fourteen? At this moment I don't really care. I have answered many of my previous questions. I have form. Pictures of my being feel as though they are unfolding through further recollections. An image at four years old opens up pictures of being five, six, and so on. But they are not complete pictures. There is no flow or consistency to them. They are fragmented snapshots. I remember them but not their history. I lack those times that made them. Nor, I might add, are they images of happiness. Even those where joy seems to have been present are tainted with a sadness that I cannot explain. A sense of belonging and yet of also not fitting into the painting. Memories are strange things indeed, especially mine.

part four

And they keep on unfolding, an infinite compendium of visualisations that carry on and on as I have unlocked some sort of box. I am partly scared, partly excited and partly confused. Where were these images coming from? What had allowed me to open them in the first place? Was it my calling that allowed me access? What about being 15, 16, 17 years old? How old am I? I allow the pictures to open themselves for my inspection. Some interest me whilst others do not. But they are flooding torrent and rapid. Often I find it hard to glimpse an image before another is layered upon it. It confuses me. My memories, the sensations the images bring become blurred and twisted and indecipherable. And still they keep coming. I want to shut my mind off. To rest and resume at a later date but the switch is stuck to 'on'. Whoever is controlling it clearly wants me to see these flashes of memory. They must also be aware that with every picture the sadness I feel grows. Paradoxically the freedom I have sought for so long is now becoming my cage. I don't want to feel these feelings, I want to escape them. My purpose was to be free not trapped within a box full of regret, sadness and pictures that are so frantic in their velocity that I can no longer see them.

Then it happens - wham! Just as I thought that I was reaching sensory overload, feeling the scream building at the back of my throat, my mind explodes as 17, 18, 19, 20, 21 years shoot me past the 14 year barrier. I feel its pain, I feel the isolation that brought me into the darkness in the first place. Deep and painful, too many for one life to bare. And now I realise why I am, or was, coated in darkness. I wonder if the Sanity Assassin was right all along. I could have had anything I wanted and I chose this. I could have had easy freedom but I chose a living hell. Everything is back with me. I have the equality that I sought. I only wish that I could loose it again. So much pain.

"Hello Melissa."

"Andrew?" I ask questioning.

"Yes, that is me. You called for your freedom, now what do you want to do with it?"

I was looking at myself within two mirrors. One placed in front of me and the other behind. I saw a man in drag and it hurt me.

"I tried to keep you out via fantasies and masturbation but, I guess, I always knew you would, in the end, be too strong for me to contain."

"Is this really me?" I ask.

"Sorry to disappoint you but yes this is us."

"I want to go back to the globe."

"To the what?"

"Never mind. What happens now?"

"Now we live with each other. We have become true to ourselves at least, or is it to ourself? I made you part of my sexual life. Dragged myself through sick and vile sexual acts just to ensnare you and dampen your spirit. But, as I have said, you were always destined to be the dominate one. This life was always meant, in a way, for you to grow."

I looked into the two mirrors again. Dragged my eyes up and down and back up again. I felt disgusted by what I saw. Where was the woman I should have grown into? All I saw was a man pretending to be female.

"Will it always be this way?" I enquire.

"It will change with treatment and time. Its not that bad."

"I hate myself," I said flatly.

"So do I, believe me, so do I"

THE MASTER OF GAMES – VIII

It was not exactly going as planned. Just as an explanation was being given to Mike ,by Claire and Andrew, Donna had called around. Mike was bewildered and Donna's face was contorted with confusion. All four of them sat outside around the table. Silence lay thick and heavy. Eyes darted from one person to another, displaying unrest, hurt and misunderstanding.

"Want to hear something funny?" Mike sneered at Donna.

"I don't know, do I? Somethings going on, what is it?"

"Ask them, they seem to know the answers," He gestured across the table to Andrew and Claire.

"Well?" Donna said.

"We, I, er, I'd rather not talk here," Andrew replied. "er, can we go somewhere. Umh, er, I need to tell you something, er, umh, shit, this is hard."

"You're sleeping with Claire," Donna said without even flinching.

"What? How did you..? What? Why do you say that?"

part four

"Just by looking at you. Both of your faces show fucking guilt. So its true, isn't it? Shit! What am I suppose to say to that? How could you do this to me?" She glared at Andrew. "I gave you everything, fucking everything. You Bastard!" She screamed, "I fucking hate you. How could you do this to me? To me for fucks sake!" She shot a glance at Mike. "Did you know?"

"Course not. I wasn't even here, was I? I know as much as you do."

Claire spoke up. "This shit really needs sorting out for us all."

"Sounds like you have already done that you bitch," Donna retorted.

"I think its time to talk straight. Talk this one out, as adults I mean."

"Fuck that," said Mike.

"Mike, just listen to what I have to say and then react, okay?"

"Just fucking make this shit quick."

And so the story unfolded slowly, interrupted by bursts of anger and irrational thought. Claire told it as it was.

She was straight, sometimes too honest. The pain her words caused were evident upon the faces and postures released by both Mike and Donna. They seemed to be hard facts to swallow. Direct and too the point. She left nothing out as the words spewed from her mouth without any regret or sorrow. Andrew looked at the faces. He felt the guilt associated with such openness. Reading the turmoil in both Donna and Mike's eyes as the story unfolded. The game, well this section, was over and Andrew had come out the loser. As far as he could see he had lost everything.

The four people remained sat around the table. Two, Claire and Andrew, were melancholy but concerned. Donna was in tears and Mike was locked in disbelief at what he was hearing. Andrew felt for them all. Things could not really have been much worse. The conversation drew on for three hours. In the end there really wasn't the need to say so much. Claire and Mike were no longer an item, Andrew and Donna were no longer together and Andrew and Claire were, simple. Ignoring feelings, this was all that was said. The outcome was equally obvious. Donna was taking it all badly. She got up to leave with tears streaming down her face. Andrew got up as well and tried to comfort her but she rejected him.

"You bastard" was about the only decipherable words. She shunned his comforting arms a second time and walked into the house. Andrew followed her through the house and out to her car. She was still crying and appeared out of control of this position.

"I hope you're fucking happy!" She blurted.

"Donna! Don't be like this. Let me explain more clearly.."

"You're fucking her aren't you?"

"Ah, yes I am."

"So, what's to say." She closed the driver's door.

"I want to say that I'm sorry and that I love you. I really am sorry."

"Shame you didn't think about that before fucking that bitch and screwing up your relationship with Mike. Fucker!"

With that she started the car and began to reverse down the driveway. Then she was gone. Andrew released his tears, slumped up against the wall of the house. He didn't try to stop the tears, they were part of his punishment. He continued to cry as he began to pull himself together and re-entered the house to see how well Claire was going. They were sitting upon the sofa, arms wrapped around each other, both also in tears. This were displays of passion that suggested a 'goodbye' rather than a 'I still love you'. Andrew entered the room and Mike looked up. Now would be the perfect time to wish the ground to open up and to swallow Andrew whole but it didn't of course and he forced to break the frustrated feelings within the room.

"Anything I can do?" He asked.

"Just leave us alone for a brief moment. There are a few things still remaining to sought out." Mike's face just read 'I hate you', so Andrew retreated back to outside and sat at the table trying to restructure his head and the game that was out of control. Somehow he felt he had to make it all him again. In the end he had decided that he didn't really trust Claire. This was especially true after the missing few hours episode whilst in Wales. He felt bad about feeling this. Especially since Claire too had sacrificed rather a lot to be with him. He felt that he should trust her, that she had done nothing really to warrant mis-trust. But, the final word rested in the pit of his stomach. He had a feeling that this relationship was as much over for him as it was for Mike and Donna. He was seldom wrong in reading his gut reaction but Andrew hoped that this would be one time when he was.

Claire was feeling guilt as she sat upon the bed talking to Mike. In three years of a relationship she had never seen him cry. She wanted to turn back the clock and restart this journey but she knew that it was far too late and, anyhow, this was her decision. She cursed Mike for crying and making her feel bad and, most of all, she cursed him for being so pathetic and non accepting of the situation. She wanted to tell him so and to finish the conversation right here and now. She drew in breath and without thinking about it, for she knew the guilt would force it to stay in, she broke the silence with words.

"Mike, there really isn't any point to this at the moment. We're not saying anything to each other, just twisting mental knifes into each other's back. I can't say anymore to you. I don't know what you want from me right now but whatever it is I can't handle it."

"Do you want me to go right now?"

"I think its best."

"There are so many things that I want to say to you but I can't get the words in my head out of my mouth. Maybe I should go. Maybe it would be better if I put some space between us for a while and talked to you at a later date."

"Maybe." She said.

Half an hour later the conversation was over and Claire left the room and stepped out into the outside. Mike disappeared upstairs quietly. She was clearly affected by her and Mike's conversation. Andrew stood up to comfort her, sensing a need to do so, but Claire rejected his advance and sat at the table where she proceeded to cry.

"How'd it go?" Andrew asked.

"Mike's leaving now. He's packing up some stuff and I said I'd send down the rest later on in the week."

"Where's he going?" Andrew held real concern within his voice.

"To his father's house. I don't know what to do about this. Shit. Its all to heavy to deal with. Can I cope without Mike?" She held her head in her hands.

Andrew sat down beside her. "This is your time Claire. You need to do this."

"Sure, sure, but the pain doesn't decrease any the less from knowing this."

"Would you like me to take him?"

"He doesn't want to see you. He's angry at you more than he is with me. Give him time. Stay here until he goes."

"I want to kiss you Claire."

part four

"I can't cope. You'll just have to wait. Sorry." She stood up and headed back inside. She turned her head. "Please stay here."

Mike left an hour later. Andrew watched through the window as they hugged for perhaps the last time. Andrew cried as he watched the scene. He knew he'd never get to explain or say goodbye to the person he considered his own flesh and blood. It was a moment worth crying for. When he had finally left Claire re-entered the house and headed straight for the sofa where she proceeded to curl up into a ball and started to cry. Andrew sat down next to her but yet again she rejected his advance.

"What's going on?" Questioned Andrew.

"In what way?"

"Your avoidance for one!"

She waved a hand in defiance and to brush off the remark. "Right now I have other things on my mind."

He left her for ten minutes and went outside again, closing the doors behind him, and sat to roll and smoke a cigarette before re-addressing Claire. When he walked back into the house he discovered that Claire had left the sofa and was now on the phone. He stopped to listen.

"You still going to invite me?...I can come this weekend.... Cheeky bastard, of course I will..." She giggled. "...only for you.....Listen, I have to go. Andrew is here at the moment and its all getting pretty heavy. I'll call you later tonight. Okay, take care honey."

They met in the dinning room. She didn't avoid him but she was clearly stand-offish. They cuddled, kissed a little, but nothing more. Andrew wanted to ask if everything was okay but he bit his tongue. It would only make things worse. Claire spent the rest of the afternoon in bed, alone, further rejecting Andrew. He had been right all along. The game was no longer his. The baton had been passed. Claire pulled the strings. She rose at around six p.m. and then drank coffee on her own before coming to sit with Andrew. The conversation was broken by long moments of silence. Not a trying silence but one they both felt was needed. The only question raised was their future. Claire was insisting that they cool it down just for a little while until she healed her relationship scars. Andrew didn't agree with this. It was out in the open so why further this charade? Her insistence won in the end. He was no match for her. The weakest always loose out to the strong.

"Will you light a fire?" Claire asked. "I need to phone someone for a second."

"Yeah, sure." He wondered if she was going to talk to the same person. Who was this person anyhow? He eavesdropped to try and find out whilst preparing the fire. He heard her pick up the phone and dial the number. A few seconds later she spoke. "Is Danny there please?" Short pause. "Hi ya honey. How's it going? Still on for tomorrow? Great, I'm looking forward to it." long pause. "I should get there mid-afternoon. Okay?" short pause. "Yeah, I'm looking forward to it too. See you tomorrow."

Suspicion, suspicious, the remnants of the conversation ran through his head. It could be nothing more than friendly banter. He would have to be on alert here. He got the fire going just as Claire entered the room.

"I'm going away for a few days tomorrow," she blatantly said.

"Fine." What else was there to say?

The rest of the night was one of occasional contact. When night drew in Claire made it clear that they would be sleeping in separate beds. Andrew lay on his realising that he was being played for a fool. He wanted to hang on to her but it wasn't his choice. As he thought about this he drifted into sleep. A sleep of nervous actions. Still, tomorrow may shed a brighter light on this although he doubted that it would.

The next morning, when Andrew arose, Claire was already up and packed. He made himself a coffee and brought it through in to the dining room. He rolled a cigarette and lit it. As he awoke Claire entered and kissed him passionately but quickly.

"What are you doing today?" Claire asked.

"Getting some stuff from the flat. You know, a few personal possessions."

"Umh," she ignored him. "I'll be back on Sunday. See you later," and then she was gone. He didn't rush. He had Danny's address and could turn up anytime he liked. He thought about the mess this was creating. A monster out of control. He had the feeling of being used in some way as if he was now a pawn. Worse still, he was becoming to view himself as a disposable piece. A sacrifice to gain a better position. He couldn't loose the thoughts. He felt so many different feelings within himself. He was scared about loosing Claire, especially after loosing Donna. Andrew vowed to speak to Donna later in the day, before heading off to Danny's house. He hoped he would be able to make amends. He began to put another game in to place. One in which Donna would come back to him. Claire was destroying him. She was better. He had compromised too much and received nothing in return. Not what he wanted, not anymore, he just wanted his life back.

THE BOOK OF HURT - Pt9

November 1999

Sunday **14**

    I became conscious yesterday after three days of sleep. I awoke to find a drip in my arm, an oxygen mask over my face and a multitude of electronics connected to me in a variety of ways. Apparently I was lucky to be alive. It is a debatable point. I, personally, would rather be dead. I don't really remember much about what happened. The trigger was just switched, at the time, I had no real control over it. At a rough guess I figure that I must have dropped 70 to 80 pills of Prozac, Diazepam, Zopiclone and anything else that was held within my bamboo box. I'd wanted to clean it out and I'm not really sure if I succeeded or not. I also remember the phone call, well sort of recall it. Why the hell had I answered it? Was it a case of backing out? I don't remember being scared at any point. I had just wanted to die. Maybe, in my loneliness, I had wanted to converse just one last time. I don't know, I don't have any knowledge, not clear anyhow, of the events. Why had I answered the phone? If only I hadn't been so stupid I would not be in any position to write this. I should be cold and stiff, upon the slab, by now with a coroner determining my cause of death. His body bent over mine as he slices my chest open to inspect my inners. Instead I had awoken in the Acute Medical Unit, alone and confused. In my semi conscious state I had just lay there cursing myself. A nurse had entered.

"Ah, good, you're awake at last," she had opened the curtains as she spoke. "You're lucky this time. We were concerned about you for a while. I'll find a doctor to see you." And then she left.

I'm lucky this time. I thought about her comment. It implied that I had not really wanted death and I wondered why she should assume this. Perhaps the phone call had made her say it. God, why was I so dumb? I should never have picked up the damn phone. Shit! Now it was too late anyhow. Ah well, another failure chalked upon the wall. Another lesson to learn from I guess. I'd fallen back to sleep only to be woken a few hours later by a doctor. It was the usual routine - I spoke to a medical doctor, the hospital psychiatrist and then my own shrink.

"Still playing games?" He'd questioned.

"No. Not playing games."

"But you want to come back to the ward, don't you? To seek attention."

"Why would I want that?" I asked.

"Because you want someone to nurture you. To take responsibility for your actions. You don't want the control."

"I'm not asking for it."

"Good, good, because you're not going to get it."

I looked at him, sitting there writing his notes. He didn't really care. He was unwilling to look beneath the action, to see the pain that I was suffering. The pain that had brought me here. He had his label for me and I was stuck with it.

This time though it had been different. There wasn't suppose to be anyone there to watch me when I fell. That was just bad luck. He'd not believe that however. I had been saved and, as far as he was concerned, I was still toying with my life merely to gather attention. He couldn't have been more wrong. I felt nothing inside. For the first time I felt as though my soul had been freed. I was empty and it felt as if nothing could fill it, not now it was too late. I had crossed a bridge. It hadn't scared me. Infact, there was a warmth sensation attached to this emptiness. A warmth that said I was nearly home.

"Do you want to talk about it? He enquired uninterested.

"Not to you, no."

"Why not to me?"

"Because you are everything I don't need. You are like these machines that are attached to me. Your job is to keep me alive and seeing as you won't truly listen to me are pointless to my life."

"Okay, you don't have to talk but I think you are being unfair to suggest I don't care. I'm here aren't I?"

"You're here because you have to be. They won't release me without my having seen you first. That's correct isn't it? A question of duty rather than of compassion."

"I can see this is getting nowhere." He stood up. "Go home, rest and think about what you did. Ask yourself why."

"Again, that's your job."

"I can't help if you reject it."

"Please, just leave me alone."

So he did. Leaving without saying another word.

"Fucker!" I cried. "Player of minds and stupid fucking games. I hate you, you bastard!"

"Hey, hey, calm down," said the nurse as she entered the room. "He's only doing his job."

"Well he's crap at it if that's the case."

"I couldn't possibly comment," she said as she looked at the chart.

Several hours later I was discharged from the Acute Medical Unit and sent home via taxi. The thought of death was still wedged within my head and was gripping like a squirrel to a tree. I had past caring about it all. Already my brain was fixed upon my next attempt. Counting up how many pills I would need to make death a reality. Part of me was annoyed. Surely they must have foreseen that I would try again or were they just idiots with no real clues. I didn't want to act so harshly but if I could see it coming then surely they must of also.

Shit, what did it matter anyhow? Their opinion meant nothing to me. It only mattered if I wanted to be saved and I didn't. I did think about what I had done though. Thought about how my family and friends would have reacted if I had of died. I was quite shocked by this. Not because of the hurt I felt but because I really didn't care. My emotions were closed. I felt nothing. Even as I write this diary entry I am emotionally sterile. Nothing grows inside of me except my concentration upon the next attempt. I am wondering how I could be so heartless and hard. I feel as if I should care and that I should realise that what I had done, and continue to do, is wrong and selfish. But, I really don't care. I can't care anymore anyway, I just want my life to be at an end. I can't even care about myself. Its kind of like being held underwater. You try to resist it, thrashing about, for a while but eventually you stop the fighting and resign yourself to your fate just to stop the fear. You welcome death as there is no other alternative.

When I had got home I had discovered that my bamboo pill box was empty. Whether I had done it or whether the paramedics had removed the remaining pills I can't be certain. One thing is for certain and that is I'll have to get some more from my doctor. I can't help wondering why, after so many failures, I still insist upon overdosing. Its painless, I suppose, that's it greatest appeal. Punctuating the really dangerous drugs with sleeping pills creates a drifting sensation that no other form of suicide can. The hanging attempt that I had tried whilst on the ward had also been painless but it had lacked any style. I guess we all have our own choice of pistol and that its familiarity creates a soothing of the soul that, I reckon, is important. I don't understand how people can be impulsive about suicide. All that panic and mixed emotions cloud the underneath. It removes the experience of calm. Calm should be present or else it merely becomes a desperate and frantic act which may cloak any regret. I have met many people who have acted in this way and the one thing that is evident in their voice is regret. I've never understood this. I have never held regret over what I have done or do. I don't see the point. Anyhow, regret merely

part four

shows that the intention is not true. Calm and collected is the only way to truly know that what you do is right.

'Free the soul - Kill the flesh'. Its that simple to me. Whether pills or razors the ideology remains the same. The razor that I have just slashed my self with a dozen times lies blood red. My left arm and both legs sing with a pleasurable pain. The lines, deep and flowing, are my sacrifice to my unknown god. They mark out a philosophy that I embrace with conviction. The blood they release helps ease tension within my head. The way it coats my flesh, before dropping on to the sheet, is my cloak of safety. Whilst I wear it nothing can touch me. Love and hate so beautifully embroided together, as one, wash through me and I welcome them both. I know that I am ill. I realise that what I do would be incomprehensible to anyone else but it doesn't matter to me. I understand what these actions mean and why I do them. I appreciate their depth and beauty and that is all that matters. No doubt there are those that would say I am deluded but they don't know. All they see is the outside and fail to appreciate the true mechanics of what I do. Their souls are too embedded for them to truly understand. They will never be free and so I don't expect them to appreciate it. Only those who have really opened themselves can relate to this.

I vowed, on the way home in the taxi, that next time I would peel back my flesh and allow my soul to fly just once more. No more fuck-ups. Next time would be final. I must give all my thoughts to this. I can hear the calling from deep within myself and know that the next act is the final one. Its cry is loud and strong, its meaning clear as the purist water. It never leaves me but nor do I want it to. We all, in the end, need a higher power to fall back on. I believe I'm lucky in that I know how to call it. How many people can place their hand on their heart and say that with any honesty?

THE MASTER OF GAMES – IX

Andrew let Claire leave the house and then followed a few hours later. Danny lived in Brighton, hip and happening, and as he drove towards it he began to realise how out of control all this had really become. The great game player turned into a quivering mess where control was non-existent. Before Claire he would have just shrugged it off and constructed a new game. However, this time he felt incapable of doing so. She had him in the palm of her hand and it was a hand that was slowly squeezing him dry. He didn't know what to do anymore. What if she is fucking Danny? What could he do about it? Yes, sure, he would be angry, but then what? Would he front it out with her? Or with him? Somehow he didn't think so. That was not his style. He didn't like conflict or violence, he was just a game player. Game players avoided such things by playing games. All this, and he was broken. As he drove passed a ten miles to Brighton signpost he wondered if his life would ever be the same again.

He inserted a tape in to the tape-player. The words were rather ironic, or so he thought at the time, and he found them swimming inside of his head. "..and by the worthy cross, would I still be soiled, when the dirt is off..." He felt that he would be. That this part of his life would carry with him forever. Andrew never realised how true a statement it was.

The car drove passed the 'welcome to Brighton' sign. He continued straight for half a mile and then turned left, followed by the second right. He was entering into Danny's road. The car slowed as he kept watch for Claire's car. He slowed a little more as he passed Danny's flat. And there it was. Parked outside upon the roadway. Gleaming in red for all to see. He pulled his car over. His heart pumping faster as he turned off the ignition and sat there.

"You bitch," He said to himself. "You fucking bitch."

He wondered what to do next. Go to the house, wait all night, leave a message so she'd know he'd been? All these possibilities and more swept through him. He lit a cigarette, thinking deeply, his ability to rationalise lost within the thick smoke. So, there he sat. Angry and hurting and trying to calm himself down. Trying to work out the most effective game he could to ensnare her and show her he'd been. But he couldn't think of one. Couldn't think past the possibility that not only had she been cheating on Mike but on him as well. Bitch. A real love square. She didn't fancy Andrew, he was just a pawn. A lever, perhaps, and the blame taker. He would be the bad person at the end of this, whilst she and Danny would come up smelling like roses. Bitch. She had played him all along. He was nothing, just a stepping stone. Andrew wondered how long she had been seeing Danny. It must have started before he and she had slept together. Maybe they were just friends and not sexual partners but he couldn't really think about it in that way.

All that trust. So much of that was to be was now lost forever. A whole future washed away by the placing of a car within a street outside a normal, Victorian house. All those dreams taken away by the Brighton tide. Carried away and tainted black. It wasn't a future he wanted to be facing. He wanted Claire. He wasn't sure if he wanted her because of all he had invested or whether it was just simply because he wanted her. He stubbed the cigarette into the ashtray and opened the door to step out. His steps onto the tarmac seemed heavy. He didn't really want to answer his questions but he just had to know. He was no joker. Andrew drew the door quickly to a close and stood there, motionless, as if time had stopped for him.

He took deep breaths to try and calm himself but the very act of being here had already shown him that he was anything but calm. The roadway was quiet. Lights from the houses were becoming beacons to be dodged. He had no intention to be seen and so kept away from their brightness. Andrew then walked up the roadway, past the house, and kept walking. When he was a few hundred yards past the house he stopped, still within the shadows, and lit another cigarette. He stood there smoking, trying to look inconspicuous, but realising that he stood out in a small thumb sort of way. He drained the last drops of nicotine from the cigarette and dropped it underfoot. He walked back the way he had came. standing there next to his car.

His urge was to mount the steps and peer into Danny's ground floor flat to see what he could gather as evidence of her crime. He just couldn't face it. Couldn't bear to realise what was happening to him. But he had to. He had to encourage himself to push onwards. He was here for a purpose not a joy-ride but a life-ride. He sat back in the car and lit another cigarette. He promised himself that he would just finish this last one and then go and see. It was the same promise he had made for the second cigarette. He re-emerged out of the car and into the night. He stood still, for a brief moment, looked up and down the road and then started upon his mission.

He reached the steps of Danny's house and paused slightly. He rechecked the status of the street and then placed his left foot upon the first step. He stopped again. Nervous energy had turned into a thumping of adrenaline. He took the second step, the third, the fourth and so on, until he reached the top step and the gloss black front door. He peered over the edge into Danny's flat, and felt his heart stop. They were there. Both upon sofa. Him and her were lying together, embracing whilst the fluorescent T.V. tube pulsated at them. Andrew felt ill. His fears were reality. Everything he had hoped wouldn't have been were now in stark reality. He wanted to scream, to bang upon the window and shout abuse but all he could do was back down the steps to the street below. He lit another cigarette whilst he gathered himself again. Thoughts of what to do next rushed through Andrew's mind. He would do them all he decided. All of his plans would screw her up, teach her a lesson.

He walked back to his car and opened the boot to draw out the 'instruments' required. Stuffing his pockets, he slammed the boot closed and checked the road yet again. He approached Claire's car, drawing out a modelling knife from his pocket as he did so. He knelt next to the car and toyed with the blade for a moment whilst reality tried to push itself inside of his head. Andrew had no time for this. The mission was paramount. She deserved this. No one fucks with Andrew, or at least no one had done so without consequence. To him, in such matters, he was the law. He sighed, lost and angry, and slid the knife in to the car's nearside front wheel. He moved to the back wheel and repeated the performance. Each stab seemed to regenerate him. By the time Andrew had done all four tyres he felt like he was floating upon air. Unstoppable, and reeling in the smell of vengeance. Fuck it! It was a dish best served cold but it worked equally well hot. He put the knife away and withdrew a nail.

Andrew looked up and down the road again but it was still quiet suburbia wrapping themselves up in quilted tranquillity for the evening. He walked to the front of the car and gripped the nail. It ran deeply and effortlessly down the side, scoring the paintwork. He walked back up again and then repeated it down the other side. He stood back to admire his handiwork. All was nearly complete. From another pocket he produced a spray can and, without a second thought, sprayed the words 'bitch' across the bonnet. Andrew drew his attention to the roof where he sprayed the simple message 'love from me'. More obscenities were inscribed upon the sides and, choosing another colour, he began to spray out the windows in electric blue.

He stepped back from the car and went back to his own. He climbed in and opened a case next to him. It contained paper and a thick marker pen. He took out the first sheet of paper and wrote 'Dear Claire, thanks for the fuck and for fucking me over. Prove its me if you can.' Andrew looked at it for a while, his anger disappearing at this point. He had done well tonight. Excessive perhaps but then this was an excessive situation. The second note was simply the word 'whore' which he then stuck blue-tac to. He ventured back up the stairs and posted the 'dear Claire' letter through the letterbox as quietly as possible. The second note he gently stuck upon the window of Danny's bedroom window. They would see it when they went off together to finalise their copulating. Bitch. As he retreated. he smiled to himself and climbed into his car. Five minutes later and he was out of Brighton. She deserved, he thought, each and every act. By tomorrow he would be gone for good and all this life would become

part four

merely memories that would fragment and fade with age. He smiled again.

FLESH OF DREAMS (8)

I open my eyes and the blackness fades into sunlight filtering in through a window. I lay there in bed, on my own, just thinking about the events of yesterday. I wanted it so much. Fell into despair over existence without ever considering the life that would await me. But then how could I have known what awaited me? I could see nothing beyond the dark. Perhaps I should have played the globe life and this life together and then made my choice. No. I concluded yesterday, after much thought, that I probably could not have broken through all the time I was still grasping to the hope of the sanity assassin and the life she offered. It was my belief in the globe that had held me back. What have I done? A nightmare awaits me. I am forced to inhabit the body imperfect for the rest of my days. I even had to sit back and watch Andrew masturbating in this very bed last night. Vile and disgusting images flowing through his mind and mine. I felt sick at how his brain worked. There could not be two more different people.

"You're awake?" Andrew enquired.

"Yes, I'm awake. Awake and disgusted by your vile mind."

"It is something you will have to put up with. I'll not go away. Not yet at least. There's still so much fun to be had."

part four

"You can not fool me," I said angrily. "I know your mind and it says that you are as disgusted by what you do and who you are as much as I am."

"Maybe. So what? I want to get to know you. To find out who you are. After all, if I am to give this body over to you, I must see that you are worthy of it." He laughed and my mind tingled.

"Maybe I don't want it." I lifted the duvet and examined the alien features. "It's not even the right sex for fucks sake!"

"Well, it's yours now. I am quite happy to just become a passenger upon this voyage. You can take the shit for a while."

I lay silent. Andrew was a fool. But what was I suppose to do? I was trapped within this mess. "I want to cry," I said.

"Fine by me. I think I would also if I were you."

So I began to cry. Releasing my first true tears. I had a feeling that it would be a performance I would repeat often in my new life. Yet, I also concluded, that I also had to make the best of a bad lot. I lay upon my side and drew my knees up to my chest as the tears continued to flow. I have had to have coped with so much already what more could dealing with this make? Best just to get on I told myself. The words of self comfort flowed like treacle but they were not as smooth. I could say them, that was easy, but even as I constructed each word I knew that I did not believe in them. I had coped before but then I had never really known what misery was. Sure, I had felt desperation in my solitude but I had always been contained by hope. Now that hope had revealed its head and what an ugly head it was. What hope was there now?

I held back the tears. "I'm not sure what to do," I said to Andrew.

"There are several options open to you. Three to be precise. Let's see. You could just live with it?"

"Not an option," I said.

"Okay. Well then, you could think about getting your body changed or, secondly, you could always top yourself."

"Kill myself you mean?"

"Yeah, why not? Plenty of people do it."

"Thanks for the help," I said sarcastically.

"Pleasures all mine."

I resumed my crying.

part four

Bastard I thought. What did he know anyway. But as the minutes ticked, I could only think about what he had said. He was right to. There were only three options. I couldn't just live with it, however, and I certainly was not about to terminate my new found freedom. That left just one choice and, as I swirled it around, I began to entertain the notion of altering this vile flesh that I saw before me. How hard could it be? I had no idea about the process involved and I wondered if Andrew might.

"I know all about it," he replied to my thought. "Come inside and have a look."

So I did. I slid my mind into his and found, much to my surprise, that not all of his thoughts were degraded or vile. He actually held information that was useful. Intellectual some might say. I wanted it.

"You can have it anytime you wish."

"Thanks."

I saw what I was after. He had amassed a fair quantity of stuff about body alterations. He was unsure what to call it. Some bits of information called it 'transsexualism', others termed it 'transgendered', whilst some referred to it as 'gender dysphoria'. It didn't matter to me. I just wanted to find out about the process. I did not care about the politics of terminology. I devoured each item, turning it over and over. Placing it against other pieces that came to light. When it was done I retreated back into my own thoughts. It seemed pretty simple from the outside.

"It's not that easy." Andrew said finally.

"Why not? Take some pills, have some surgery, buy new clothes. Sounds fairly easy."

"Do you want to know more?"

"Okay. But tell me. I can't be bothered to trawl through your mind again."

"Right. Well, firstly, there's the issue of having to see a doctor, then a specialist, then they both have to agree with you..."

"What's it got to do with them?"

"Who's gonna perform the surgery? Do you think that you can just pick a surgeon and get it done?"

"Can't I?" I enquired.

"No. Just listen for a while. Okay? You'll probably need counselling as well. That will all give you a vagina, of sorts, but then you have to go through the whole process again to have breast surgery. You'll have to get referred

part four

to a consultant for hormone replacement. Then, what else? Oh yeah. What about the voice? I like mine but I'm sure it doesn't suit you. You also have to learn about clothes, about deportment, about changing your name. Shall I go on?"

"No. No more." I straightened out my body. "I don't really understand why its so hard. How long will it take?"

"A couple of years if you are lucky. If not, anything up to ten years."

"A decade!" I exclaimed.

"Yeah, maybe. And lets not forget about the money it will cost."

"Money?"

"Yep. You'll probably have to pay for some, or all, of this treatment."

"How much will it all cost?"

"If you have to pay for it all then around ten thousand pounds."

"What!"

"Thought about a job?" he laughed.

"No, I haven't. I should have taken the globe life after all." I said reaching despair again.

"What is this globe?" he asked.

"Oh, nothing. You'll find out later."

"Another thing for you to consider is how people will react to you wandering around in women's clothes."

"But I am a woman."

"You might be but its my body remember?"

"Will they notice?"

"I'm six foot two."

"So what?"

"It's rather tall for a woman."

"Oh right. Will I get beaten up?"

"Shit happens."

part four

I've reached the bottom. I feel as if I am floating within poisoned air. I try to breath but find it laboured and hard. The thought of ten years worth of beatings and ridicule lie at the fore-front of my thoughts. How do people cope with this? Surely I am not the only one to have to go through this situation? It offers little comfort to me however. I am beginning to feel depressed at what lays ahead. Trying to retract back into my mind I find its pathway blocked by Andrew. I force myself harder but his barriers hold tight.

"This is my place now Melissa," He sneers outloud. You can face it from now on. I'm merely an on-looker. Just having thoughts and occasionally fucking your life up as you did to me."

"I'm begging you!"

"Don't care. I'm over 30 years old. Do you know how much pain you can amass in 30 years?"

"No. But I think I'll find out if I live that long."

"Sure you will."

"I can't do this," I sighed again.

"You've no choice, if that is your option."

"Why is it so hard?"

Andrew smiled, long and hard, and then released a breath that I had fought so hard to in-take.

"Welcome to the real world."

His laughter sliced me like a knife and I felt my heart begin to bleed.

"Welcome to the real world. You have no idea what it has in store."

THE BOOK OF HURT – Pt10

November 1999

***Wednesday* 17**

Today I had to see my psychiatrist at the day clinic. I hadn't slept with dread. I didn't like his implications at the last meeting we had. How could an over dose be a game? I am still baffled by this and yet his comments that day still haunt me in my waking hours. I couldn't explain why, I don't believe his words to be true, I think its because my carer seems not to care. If he can't understand me then what hope is there for me? I took all this to the appointment. Sitting there with sweaty palms and a throat as dry as the Arizona desert. I'd tried not to think about anything as I waited but these words twisted through my blanket with ease. Then I'd seen him, walking up the corridor towards me, with his usual smile-free expression. I'd thought about running but I couldn't move from my chair.

"Hi Mel," he'd said disinterested.

"Hello."

"Follow me please."

I made sure I was walking behind him. I hadn't wanted him to observe me anymore than was really necessary. He opened a door, I followed, into a room where a desk, two chairs, a bookcase crammed with books and a rather ill pot-plant greeted me.

"Sit down."

Whilst removing my coat I had actually thought about asking him how he was. I'm glad I hadn't now. I seated myself and waited for the slaughter to begin. He started the conversation, perhaps seeing that I wouldn't.

"So, how do you feel after the overdose attempt?"

"Alright, I guess. I have my faith to see me through."

"Ah, yes," he'd opened my file, rummaged through a few pages, read something and then looked at me again. "What does 'free the soul and eat the flesh' mean?"

"It means what it says. I will free my soul by killing or eating away at my flesh. Its a simple philosophy but I like it."

"Umh. Was it this thought that made you take the pills?"

"Yeah. Why is that a problem?"

"Do you want it to be?"

I'd gasped. "Not this game playing shit again," I'd said.

"It was just a question, you don't need to answer it if you do not wish to. What else have you been doing since you left the ward? Can you tell me about this?"

"Not much really. I still can't function and do all the normal day to day things. I just don't want to go on with life at the moment. What hope is there for someone like me? I'm as depressed as fuck and I don't think that anyone really cares. Well, maybe that's a bit harsh. I guess that I'm trying to say that I feel alone with this problem. I'm scared of the helpers."

He'd sat forward at this point as if actually interested in my ramblings. It made me fall silent again. My chain of thought broken by his action.

"You said '..go on with life at the moment..'. So you actually want something better than what you think you have now. That is encouraging to hear. Why are you scared of my staff and I?"

"You are the controllers of my destiny, that is why."

"I can not stop you taking your own life if that is what you wish to do. But, ask yourself, is that really what you want to do to yourself?"

"It is what my belief tells me is the correct way. What I want doesn't really come into it."

After scribbling something down he'd turned to face me again.

"I don't understand something. I hope you can explain it to me, if you don't mind. You created this belief yourself, so surely you have decided that this is to be your course of action."

I hadn't expected him to understand.

"No." I'd replied. "It has always been inside of me. All I had to do was to look deeply and listen to what my soul was saying. Its much wiser than me, it tells me the direction and I just follow.

"Umh," he'd said again. "continue please."

And that is how it did continue. Three quarters of an hour's worth of talk. He had summed it all up with a 'I'll see you in a week' gesture and I had been left still without any real conclusion to what was going on. As I drove back from this meeting I chanted my mantra over and over within my head. As I was doing so a thought had occurred to me. Why was I bothered about discovering any conclusion? It doesn't make any difference to how I feel and to what course of action I take. During my discussion with the

part four

psychiatrist I had been waiting for him to say 'ah I see, I think that you have this wrong with you.' But he didn't. I was disappointed. Now I'm confused. Perhaps I do want to get better.

Nah! that's stupid. I wouldn't have taken the pills so many times if that was the case. I wouldn't be saving up my pill supply again if that were true. I reckon I just need to stop thinking about it so much. Thought only killed good action. I could think my way out of doing anything if I wanted to. That only serves to show how weak-willed I am. Some things are best left alone and just acted out rather than chewed over and then spat out, filled with remorse.

THE MASTER OF GAMES – X

After the events of Brighton Andrew returned back to Carey's house. As the key turned in the door lock the realisation of his actions struck him motionless for a brief moment. A thousand fragmented thoughts fought for possession of his mind's central chamber but he could hold on to none of them for any length of time. He shook his head to clear it and continued twisting the brass key. The lock retracted and the door opened to a blackened room that had once held his laughter. He stepped into the room, fumbling for the light switch and an end to his gloomy thoughts. His fingers touched at the panel and the false daylight instantly sparked in to life. The brightness brought a new vision in to his thoughts. Here he was in the very place where it had all started. His gaze fell desperately on to familiar items as Andrew tried to recapture the moment. But his enthusiasm had gone. He no longer had the appetite to cherish the time. What he saw surrounding him was no longer a part of his dream but a part of his nightmare.

Andrew slumped in to a chair, fumbling with his house key, mind awash and with eyes that gazed blankly. He had to leave this place. Had to just leave the key, turn out the lights and close the door to this particular element of his life. Yet, despite the actions of the night and the feelings he held, there was a reluctance to do so. There had been great investment made and Andrew felt like he should have some return on it. It was a stupid notion. Claire would never again step in to his life as she had, not now, that was no longer an option. He cursed his deed and wondered if it would have all been better if he had not gone to Brighton at all.

Andrew replayed what he had seen in Danny's flat. The two of them embracing each other, Claire clearly without thought for Andrew's pain. It would never be the same. Bitch. She had destroyed him. There was a strength in this realisation and he allowed himself to feed off it. He stood up and began to recover the few meagre possessions that lay scattered around. He placed them upon the table, one by one, and then proceeded in to the sitting room to repeat the process. Bit by bit he began to erase his presence within the brick structure, placing each piece, like a prize, upon the table.

He flicked the hallway light on and climbed the steps to the upstairs bedrooms. He stopped off in the bathroom first and collected his wash items. Stuffing them within a washbag. As he exited Andrew threw the washbag down to the bottom of the stairs. It bounced off the last two steps, rebounded off the end wall and came to rest. He then entered in to what had been, last night at least, 'his' bedroom. Feeling a sense of hurt and regret entwined he did not dwell. His few possessions were gathered up quickly and, like the washbag, were deposited at the foot of the stairs. He turned off the light and stepped across the hall to face Claire's room.

The door to her room was closed. Andrew just stood there staring at the pine blockade. He imagined the inside and the two of them laughing and sprawled out upon the bed. "Forget it," he told himself. But he replayed it one more time, "just for old time's sake."

Twisting the knob, the door released its lock. It swung open slightly and then stopped, leaving a gapping crack. Andrew brought up his right foot and slammed it in to the pine. The door flew open, rebounded off its hinges, closed again and then opened fully. The light brought his memories back, leaving him silent and still. He scanned the room picking out his items. Clothes, books, a candle, a collection of photographs and his wooden bamboo box. Making no attempt to collect them, he stood as if stone. Another door opened and Andrew spun around, panicked. Carey stood, rubbing her eyes, in the hallway. Her dressing gown was undone and her hair lay to one side.

"Claire?" She asked dreamily.

"No, its me."

"Oh! What's going on? I was asleep."

"Sorry Carey. I'm just gathering a few things and then I'll be on my way. I'll leave the key before I go."

Carey awoke a little more. "What's up?" She said as she tied the dressing gown.

"Claire."

"Not you as well! What has she done now?"

Andrew stepped towards Carey a little more.

"She's fucking Danny as well as me."

"Oh, I'm sorry. Do you want to talk about it?"

Andrew liked Carey. In all the years he had known her she had always been honest and compassionate to others. He shrugged, as if unsure how to answer her question.

"Let's have a cup of tea and a joint," she said. "Get it off your chest."

"I'm not sure that..."

"Do it for me, if not for you."

Andrew gave in. He followed her downstairs and went in to the kitchen whilst Carey sat at the dinning room table. They never spoke until Andrew emerged carrying two steaming cups. Carey had a half-rolled joint upon the table top, which she was ignoring for the present, and was looking at the tape box.

"I love this tape," she finally said.

"Have it. Take it as a gift or something."

"Yeah? Thanks. Put it on will you."

Carey passed it over and resumed with the joint. As Andrew put the tape in to the player he considered the chance of getting Carey in to bed. That would really piss Claire off. Making love to her mother would make her furious. He pressed play and turned around. He looked at Carey. "No more games," he thought, "Carey doesn't deserve this."

He sat down instead and began to re-tell the past events. He asked her if Claire had phoned her whilst they were in Wales.

"No," was all she replied.

"I knew she was lying. That was really the first doubt I had."

"She has been phoning Danny a lot in the past couple of months." Carey stopped to light the joint. "You don't think she was sleeping with Mike, you and Danny all at the same time. Do you?"

"Yeah, it seems likely."

"Jesus shit."

"How do you think I feel?"

They sat there for hours. Daylight was entering the room as the conversation concluded. Andrew was surprised that, although Carey remained loyal to Claire, she was also angry at her actions. He neglected to tell Carey about the car damage but she would find out from Claire, Andrew concluded, and then that would be another friend lost. With Carey's help, he had collected and bagged the rest of his things and prepared himself to leave before Claire called telling Carey about the car.

He stood upon the doorstep.

"Take care," Carey said bending forward and kissing Andrew on the cheek. "I don't suppose you'll be around here again?"

"I don't suppose I will."

"Shame. I'll miss you."

"Thanks Carey." Andrew opened his car door and threw in the bags. "See you around." With that he got in, started the engine and headed for home.

Talking to Carey had not really helped. His flat felt empty as he sat there wondering what to do next. What a mess! Andrew knew that he had lost a lot in this. And his first impression of the affair had been right. Namely that Claire and Danny would come out of this smelling sweetly, whilst he would be portrayed as the villain. He felt trapped within a corner. "Stupid," continually entered his mind, "fucking stupid."

After several hours reflection Andrew had concluded that he had to escape from this scene totally. He would pack up a few important and necessary items and get the hell out of town, for good if possible. There really was not a lot of choice. He stuffed things in to bags. Took some food, clothes, music, a paraphernalia of small items and a few books. As he searched through his wardrobe Andrew came across the suitcase the sat upon the base of the unit. He flicked the catches and examined the clothing. He wondered if he should take some of them with him. As Andrew toyed with this notion he began to undress and put on some of the suitcase's contents. Once completed, he decided that he really couldn't do without them. He turned to face himself in the mirror. The second mirror, behind him, gave him two views of his true self. The self that had no one had ever known. He began to masturbate.

THE BOOK OF HURT – Pt11

November 1999

Sunday **21**

    I've just written and posted my final letter and now I am writing my final diary entry. Its kind of hard to know what to say at this point in time. I've said all along that I couldn't cope with all this and that I hate who I am and what I have become. I really can't put up with it anymore. What sort of life is it that I live? I spend all my days in a drug trance, sitting around the house crying or thinking about death. Now its coming to an end. I can only take consolation in the fact that it is an end that I create. In this respect, it is something that I want to do.

When I started this journey I never ever thought that I would end up like this. I thought that it would all work out in the end. I knew it would be hard but I went through so much to get here. Went through the specialists, the voice therapy, the hormones, the surgery, all of it. Years and years of my life were invested in the process of changing Andrew into Melissa. Yet, I never really had any choice. Melissa couldn't be contained any longer and Andrew was just a vile and disgusting game player anyway who wasn't worth pissing on.

I can only send my love and regards to my family. I am as sorry for them as I am for myself - perhaps more so. They have supported me constantly throughout all of this. Now they will suffer in the wake of my death. I really am sorry to put you all through this. I hope you can realise that it is, in the end, all for the best. I love you all.

I am fed up with taking ill-fated overdoses, so I've made sure that this time there can be no turning back. God! I hope not anyway. Going through all this just to end up in the Acute Medical Unit again would be too much to handle. But I'm pretty sure that it won't happen anyhow. I've managed to obtain some liquid morphine, to help with the sleeping, which is much better than pills. I'll take this whilst inhaling the fumes from my car exhaust - all of which should finish me off. Desperate times call for very desperate measures.

So, these are my last words. There is nothing more to say except for those words that, in a way, have come to haunt me as much as comfort. 'Free the soul and eat the flesh.' My body will prove its dedication through its eradication. My soul shall be free at long last and I shall live the life that I was destined to do. There can be nothing more than this. This is all I am.

Goodbye.

FREAK UNIQUE

freak - freak
freak - unique
people laughing - tongue in cheek
gazing - amazing - widened eyes
at the portrayal - that herein lies
prodded - pokered - touching flesh
the show's in town - and in Sunday best
they stare with faces - show fascination
at this strange un-godly creation
lying bare - for all to see
10,000 images all of me
penis - breasts - warts and all
seemingly open for public call
no shivering corner - can thus defend
when chained so central - but to make amends
is blind-folded from seeing the gathering below
but for a few shillings more - a private show
is arranged in a backroom - no questions asked
violated body and tattered mask
bleeding wounds - a face of hurt
displayed as kneeling in the dirt
violence - violation - continues again
and outside - in his dreams - the pouring rain
washes these memories and wipes them clean
showing him pictures of what might have been
and then its over - in black of night
he trembles and cries at the mental sight
projected - replayed - in constant time
he lies in the dirt - with the shit and the grime
freak - freak - freak - unique
there is no place upon this street
for you and your disgusting ways
we are harping back to the halcyon days

the crying shore

where within the streets children played
not preyed upon - but just stayed
where they can grow in innocence - as they do with age
but for every ten of them - one has a cage
freak - unique - tongue in cheek
look around before you speak
the truth is sharp and hard to bare
but near or beside you we are there
hidden and cloaked and screaming inside
in this place you force us to hide

DAWNING AND MOVING

what is the time
is it slowly dawning
will I wake up
to a sun drenched morning
and to yet another crime
that leaves me yawning
been there before
and have seen the warning
flashing in colours
of blue and a red
as the pain increases
within my head
I've begged and I've borrowed
just to achieve my releases
cried with deep sorrow
and then picked up the pieces
and stored them away
back into their niches
just to move onward
I perform these tasks
neatly hidden
behind a smiling mask
and I wonder quite often
how long it lasts
and I raise my head
as I raise my glass
to drink to a freedom
that may come my way
I am counting the seconds
without any delay
what is the time
is it slowly dawning
am I merely dreaming of my perfect morning

www.ingramcontent.com/pod-product-compliance
Lightning Source LLC
Chambersburg PA
CBHW071222080526
44587CB00013BA/1461